D1484654

WRITE THE SAT ESSAY RIGHT!

Ten Secrets to Add 100 Points to Your Score

Write the SAT Essay Right! Ten Secrets to Add 100 Points to Your Score

© 2010 Laura Wilson. All Rights Reserved.

Cover design: Studio Montage

Back cover, book layout, and design: Marble Sharp Studios

Editor: Tiffany Morgan

Maupin House publishes professional resources for K-12 educators. Contact us for tailored, in-school training or to schedule an author for a workshop or conference. Visit www.maupinhouse.com for free lesson plan downloads.

Library of Congress Cataloging-in-Publication Data

Wilson, Laura, 1964-

Write the SAT essay right! : ten secrets to add 100 points to your score / Laura Wilson. -- Teacher/trade ed.

p. cm.

ISBN 978-1-934338-78-0

1. English language--Composition and exercises--Examinations--Study guides. 2. SAT (Educational test)--Study guides. I. Title.

LB2353.57.W56 2010b

378.1'662--dc22

2010023762

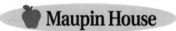

Maupin House Publishing, Inc.
2416 N.W. 71st Place
Gainesville, FL 32653

www.maupinhouse.com

800-524-0634
352-373-5588
352-373-5546 (fax)
info@maupinhouse.com

10 9 8 7 6 5 4 3 2 1

DEDICATION

To all my students, who continue to inspire me.

ACKNOWLEDGMENTS

The completion of this book would not have been possible without the expertise, enthusiasm, and wonderful "voice" of Amie Whigham. Thank you, Amie.

I would also like to gratefully acknowledge all others who have contributed to this book and helped turn my idea into a reality. First, to my tireless agent, Marie Rama.

Also, a special thanks to my extraordinary verbal tutors, Melissa Slive, Amy Friedlander, Ellen Stein, and Vicki Rushworth for their insightful contributions. And also to P.K. Shiu, Laura Cacciato, Sue and Jim at Mount Kisco Printing, and all others who helped me along the way.

TABLE OF CONTENTS

INTRODUCTION

Pssst . . . over here. I've got a secret . . . . Actually, I've got ten secrets. And, lucky for you, I'm a blabbermouth. I'm revealing each and every essay-writing secret so that you can add 100 points to your SAT writing score.

This book gives you the secrets—the secret ingredients, the secret formula, the secret weapons—for writing a powerful, persuasive, on-the-spot essay. From approaching the essay to taking a position, to writing an introduction, body, and conclusion, this book reveals the "magic" behind top-scoring essays.

Don't worry—there are no sleights of hand or fancy mirror tricks involved—just a few little-known tips that can transform an average essay into an awesome essay, regardless of how unsure you are of your writing ability.

I'll serve as your behind-the-scenes coach. However, coaching is a two-person job: it requires a coach and a player. The coach may prepare the player, but it is the player's job to practice. I'll be here to guide, to assist, and to motivate, but you have to do the work. I'll reveal to you the secrets of SAT essay writing, but you have to utilize these secrets. You have to execute the strategies and apply the skills you learn. With a little effort, you can make these secrets your own.

The secrets I reveal—and the key strategies I introduce— outline the steps you need to create a compelling, unconventional essay in, yes, only twenty-five minutes. You will arrive at the test confident, in control, and ready to answer any essay question thrown at you.

The SAT encourages formulaic writing. This book includes the secret formula needed to achieve a high-scoring SAT essay.

As you read through this book, look in the margins for extra help: key strategies, marked with a skeleton key, pull out important ideas to commit to memory; sticky notes draw your attention to essential SAT facts; and highlighted text blocks serve to underscore important points.

Although twenty-five minutes of writing followed by hours of multiple-choice questions may not make for the perfect Saturday morning, I'll prove to you that the essay is a fantastically easy way to rack up points on the SAT. So roll up your sleeves, crack your knuckles if you're looking for added effect, and put the pencil to the pad. It's time to *Write the SAT Essay Right*.

Note: All essays within this book are actual essays written by students and may contain grammatical errors. Spelling has been corrected for ease of reading.

"Chance favors the prepared mind."
LOUIS PASTEUR, FRENCH CHEMIST/MICROBIOLOGIST

CHAPTER 1

ANSWER THE QUESTION BEFORE TEST DAY

The bell rings. Thirty-four English notebooks close simultaneously. Thirty-four chairs slide out from under desks across a linoleum floor. Conversation erupts and the students hastily make their way toward the door. "And class, don't forget your essays are due next Monday!"

No teacher ever yells, "And class, don't forget your essays are due in exactly twenty-five minutes!" A twenty-five minute, on-the-spot essay is an unheard of and seemingly impossible assignment—but this is exactly what the SAT requires you to do.

Brainstorming, writing, and editing a complete essay, including an introduction, supporting body paragraphs, and a conclusion, all in response to an indecipherable, esoteric* quote in only twenty-five minutes—*legibly*—may seem an outrageous assignment. But to all you anxiety-ridden high-school juniors out there, stop biting your fingernails! *Write the SAT Essay Right* will melt away the stress of test day.

*ESOTERIC
Hard to understand

DON'T PANIC!

By now in your high-school career, you know what to do when you're given an essay assignment. After all, you've composed not just one, but probably a hundred different responses. You're trained and brainwashed to know the structure of an essay: *intro, thesis, body, conclusion . . . intro, thesis, body, conclusion . . . .*

English class has turned you into an essay-writing machine, giving you the necessary foundational skills. For classroom essay assignments, you discuss the essay with your peers, brainstorm, write, edit, erase, add, edit, shake your head, erase again, add a little more, and *shazaam*: an A+ composition. If you're working alone, follow the secrets and practice.

Now it's time to oil the gears, kick it up a notch, and write a three-day assignment in only twenty-five minutes! This same process (aside from the discussing with your peers!) will happen on test day, but it takes place in something of a time warp.

In only twenty-five minutes, you must come up with your idea, develop one or two (two is definitely better!) points, and create a well-organized, grammatically correct, proofread essay. Now, I know you are thinking that this is a hopeless situation and that you will never be able to do all this in twenty-five minutes.

Well, you're right! It is a hopeless situation, and you will never be able to do everything in twenty-five minutes. But you're not going to be limited to only twenty-five minutes.

So here's what you are going to do: you're going to prepare ahead of time and write your essay before you ever show up at the exam.

SECRET #1

YOU CAN ANSWER THE QUESTION BEFORE TEST DAY!

Secret # 1 is the secret of all secrets. A pre-written essay is your ultimate goal.

The goal is simple: pre-write your SAT essay response, perfect it, and then spit it out on test day. To do this, though, you need the remaining secrets. With each secret, you'll be one step closer to composing an above-average response before you ever see the SAT essay assignment.

Preparing your response ahead of time is the number one secret, the number one goal, the number one priority in SAT essay writing. Why? Because on-the-spot SAT responses tend to be vague, superficial, and—at best—loosely organized. You're going to avoid these superficial, pedestrian* compositions by writing your response before test day. You're not going to write an essay like everyone else because your essay is not going to earn an average score. Your essay will be better and will earn you an above-average score.

*PEDESTRIAN
Average

The SAT is standardized, meaning that it's graded on a normal (bell) curve. Since the maximum score is 12, the bulk of the scores, then, will be 6s, 7s, and 8s—in short, average! Trite!* Banal*! This is because it's difficult to add depth and development without knowing the question beforehand—especially if the essay has to be written in twenty-five minutes.

*TRITE
Lacking freshness
*BANAL
Overused

Graders read hundreds of essays, all of which start to sound the same. Therefore, they all get the same score. If you want above an 8 (which I'm sure you do), you need to take control: don't sound like everybody else!

Now, there is nothing wrong with average. But, with just a little work, my goal is for you to score a 9 or higher on this essay. Why? Because a 9 or higher will dramatically increase your SAT score. The essay accounts for one-third of your writing component score. A multiple-choice score of 500 and an essay score of 10 results in a combined writing score of 600. An 11 on the essay, and that's boosted to a 620. A perfect essay score of 12 brings it up to a 630. SAT composite score conversion tables are established for each SAT by the College Board. Exact score combinations will vary from test to test.

The SAT Essay is graded separately by two readers and scored out of 6 points. Their scores are then combined for a maximum essay score of 12. The national average is a 7.

So, although there's nothing wrong with average, it's better to score above average and get those extra hundred points!

The essay can add an additional 100 points to your multiple-choice writing score.

My goal is to help you break out of mainstream writing, prove your point, and enter into extraordinary writing.

Take a look at the following three essays written in response to the following SAT essay prompt: *"Tough challenges reveal our strengths and weaknesses.*" *This statement is certainly true. Adversity helps us discover who we are. Hardships can often lead us to examine who we are and to question what is important in life. In fact, people who have experienced seriously adverse events frequently report that they were positively changed by their negative experiences.*

ASSIGNMENT: *"Do you think that ease does not challenge us and that we need adversity to help us discover who we really are?"*

I believe that it is true that adversity shows us who we really are. We do not know what we are truly like until we face some sort of hardship. Sometimes people discover that they are cowards. Other times people become heroes.

Martin Luther King, Jr. discovered that he was a hero when he was faced with adversity. After slavery ended, Black Americans suffered a lot and were segregated and oppressed. During the Civil Rights movement, Blacks started boycotting and protesting this oppression. One of these protesters was Martin Luther King, Jr. He fought hard for his people, demanded equality, and as a result, was assassinated.

Jewish people during the Holocaust also faced much adversity. During WWII in Germany, Hitler moved all of the Jewish population into concentration camps, where he basically tortured them. The Jewish people tried to stick together and help each other, but millions of people were killed during the Holocaust.

Adversity can bring out the best in people and prove that they are strong. Martin Luther King, Jr. and the Jewish victims of the Holocaust are examples that show that "Ease does not challenge us."

SCORE: 6
RATING: Average

Most likely, you can hear yourself in this essay. It's not the worst essay, but it's certainly not the best essay either. In fact, it's right in the middle: average.

This student followed the general "brainwash" formula of expository writing but lacked the detail and development necessary to attain a top score. The essay mentions two examples of people who faced adversity, but it does not develop these examples, nor does it really get into the "meat and potatoes" of the question. Both Martin Luther King, Jr. and the Holocaust are addressed superficially.

As a result, this essay fails to address the complexity of the essay prompt. In other words, *how does adversity foster growth and knowledge*? How has society learned from the atrocities and prejudices suffered by Martin Luther King, Jr. and the victims of the Holocaust?

The superficiality of this essay most likely is the result of having to recall dates, details, and specifics off the cuff. Clearly, no one let this student in on Secret #1. Alas, a not-so-special essay.

The following is a more fully developed response to the same essay question. The introduction is much stronger, and the essay is organized with transitional and topic sentences. However, as you'll soon read, the examples chosen aren't superb.

Adversity. The challenges we face day to day— economically, politically and personally—can make or break us. But whether it shows us to be a hero or a coward, adversity puts us to the test and reveals our true colors. Martin Luther King, Jr. rose above the oppression of African Americans and demanded equality. The victims of the Holocaust, tortured and tormented, banded together and survived as a group.

Slavery had ended a century prior, but the aftermath of such institutionalized racism weighed heavily upon

Martin Luther King, Jr. His entire life, King had been refused, denied and shut out because of his skin color. Segregation and bigotry in his Southern home were flaring out of control, and in the midst of hatred, violence and prejudice, King took a stand. He refused to be stamped out by the White population, and with a powerful voice, demanded justice and equality for all, regardless of race. He became the face of the Civil Rights Movement, and through protests, boycotts and other peaceful measures, King moved the Black population one step closer to equality. Faced with innumerable disadvantages, King became a hero.

Prejudice is seen in all forms, and is not limited to race. Led by Adolf Hitler in the 1940s, Germany enforced genocide, attempting to eradicate the Jewish population of Europe. Hitler's plan was formulaic: first, he identified Jews by requiring a sign-in sheet at every synagogue. He then demanded that Jews be "labeled," requiring that they wear a Star of David patch on their clothing at all times. Steadily, Hitler moved to more drastic measures, closing down shops, imprisoning and interrogating Jews, and hoarding them into concentration camps where they were tortured and executed. The unfathomable adversity of the Holocaust showed that the Jewish population refused to sacrifice their religious beliefs or integrity.

Adversity can bring out the best in people, and reveals courage and strength. Martin Luther King, Jr. and the countless victims of the Holocaust found their strength when challenged with adversity.

SCORE: 9
RATING: Almost There

Again, the above essay is good, impressive even, but it could be a lot more impressive had it mentioned different examples. Many students choose to write about Hitler, the Holocaust, and Martin Luther King, Jr., as all of these are high-school history milestones—and they are the first things that come to mind under time-pressure situations. But, there are many other people and events that shaped World War II and the Civil Rights Movement that will help you write a thoughtful essay that stands out from the crowd.

Also, note that this essay, like the first one, fails to address the complexity of the prompt: how adversity can promote growth and self-discovery.

This third essay, however, does fully address the essay question. No longer pedestrian, this essay has the detail and style needed to impress the graders. The examples are specific and novel, the vocabulary is strong, and the writing is cohesive. This essay would receive a 12—a perfect score.

Use detail and style to impress the graders!

In light of the terrorist attacks on September 11th, many have called the last few years a defining moment in American history. Suddenly, the apathetic society of the 1990s has been shaken out of its complacency, and in response to the threat, those who had quipped "whatever" are now crying out "freedom!" Indeed, in this way, "Ease does not challenge us, but adversity shows us who we really are." This is seen consistently throughout history, including during WWII and the American Civil Rights Movement.

During WWII, the British people faced a constant struggle near to their hearts. While the Germans bombed London almost daily, the population was forced to hide out in subterranean subway stations. At this point, with their shops, homes and city being destroyed, it would have been easy for the English to give up. However, they refused to give in and fought back. When the Royal Air Force was finally able to push the Nazi regimes out of the British Isles, it was evidence of the courage and perseverance of the British people.

The British people's strength was tested and they responded courageously and with integrity, refusing to give in. In times of peace and ease it is easy to assume oneself brave—but when push came to shove the British proved that they were indeed more than an assumption; they were brave.

Just as the British were faced with daily adversity during WWII, African Americans struggled daily during the Civil Rights Movements of the 1960s. African Americans were faced with the daily decision of whether to continue their struggle for equality or to accept life as it was— oppressive and segregated. Through court decisions, "sit-ins" and "hosings," the decision was never easy. It was only through constant determination and the will to prevail that the African Americans truly understood themselves. The odds were against them, and history had shown the whites successful at oppressing them as a group for hundreds of years, but they had the courage to move forward, demanding change. With the leadership of Martin Luther King, Jr. and the controversial support of others, such as Malcolm X, African Americans made progress. These leaders, and many others, formed the heart and soul of the Civil Rights Movement, one that refused to give in. Although constantly faced with naysayers, the African American community went through a period of self-understanding, only then able to succeed.

In both cases, the British and the African Americans, the people involved did not truly understand themselves until faced with extreme adversity. Everyone is faced with a challenge at some point in their lives, and each group will respond in a different way. But if we learn from the challenge, and grow through struggle, then even if we fail it will not have been for nothing.

SCORE: 12
RATING: Awesome

This essay truly develops, analyzes, and answers the essay question: how does adversity show us who we really are? It compares and contrasts adversity to ease, shows how adversity forces people into action, and does so by using specific examples and details.

Rather than writing a general overview of the Holocaust, the essay addresses a different, specific event within that time period. The conclusion broadens the essay to encompass not only history, but also the present day, and it ends powerfully. Obviously, this student was prepared ahead of time (and was in on the rest of the hush-hush contained in this book).

This essay has the structure, substance, and style necessary to hook a reader, keep that reader engaged, and leave a lasting impression. And, with the help of this book, so will yours!

Each of the following chapters reveals the secrets and develops the skills needed to perfect the SAT essay. Remember, Secret #1 is to do all the legwork before you arrive on test day.

So bring it on, SAT. With this book, you'll be ready!

Use the secrets revealed in this book to write your essay before test day.

CHAPTER 2

LEARN THE FIFTEEN QUESTIONS ALWAYS ASKED

So, now that I've told you to go beyond what you have learned in English class, the SAT is looking a little scary.

You fear not knowing how to answer the question, and spending fifteen minutes thinking of a response and only having ten minutes left to write an answer. You're afraid of not being able to think of any examples to support your answer, and not being able to organize your thoughts coherently in twenty-five minutes.

These fears are valid, but they are easily conquered. Besides, the essay has no teeth, no claws, and no poisonous stinger, so you'd *totally* win in a fight. Plus, aside from being almost completely harmless (there's always the lingering threat of a paper cut), there's a solution . . . Secret #2.

SECRET #2

YOU CAN PREDICT THE SAT ESSAY QUESTION!

I'm not talking psychic powers, Magic 8 Ball, or voodoo. I'm talking patterns: the SAT essay is completely predictable.

Each SAT essay presents you with a quotation (often a confusing background paragraph or literary excerpt) coupled with a straightforward assignment. These assignments repeat from test to test. Notice how verbose* the following quote is and how clear the assignment question is.

VERBOSE
Wordy

For example:

It is unrealistic to think that any group of people—a family, a committee, a company, a city—can function peacefully and productively without some kind of authority. The needs and interests of the individuals who make up any group are too varied for its members to operate as a unit without having someone to make the final decisions. Somebody has to be in charge; somebody has to be ultimately responsible.

ASSIGNMENT: *"Can a group of people function effectively without someone being in charge? Plan and write an essay in which you develop your point of view on this issue. Support your position with reasoning and examples taken from your readings, studies, experience, or observations."*

After studying countless SAT questions, I discovered a secret: the essay questions repeat. The SAT literally asks the same questions from year to year, reworded in a slightly different fashion. The above question ("Can a group function peacefully/effectively?") happens to revolve around a common theme: cooperation vs. competition. In fact, with rare exceptions, every SAT essay question relates to one of fifteen predictable themes.

Focus on the essay assignment. Do not worry about addressing the excerpt.

Knowing these themes—the core topics, as I call them—will give you an advantage on test day because you'll walk in knowing exactly what to expect. Knowing what to expect brings you that much closer to writing your essay before test day.

FIFTEEN CORE TOPICS

- choices
- competition vs. cooperation
- conflict
- conscience/ethics
- creativity
- group vs. individual
- happiness
- heroism
- motivation
- perfection
- perspective/truth
- sacrifice/suffering
- success
- technology/change
- wisdom

These fifteen core topics must be memorized. I've added a core topic reminder sheet on p. 16, so photocopy it and keep it handy. Look at it. Stare at it. Memorize these topics!

Realize that these are called core topics—and not "directly stated, word-for-word assignment" topics—for a reason. These core topics revolve around central themes. Your job is to reduce the convoluted, complicated craziness (a little alliteration from my English teaching days!) to one of the fifteen core topics. To do so, it is imperative on test day that you circle the key words within the essay assignment and that you define these key words in your introduction. The key words are those that relate directly to one the fifteen core topics.

For instance, a question about knowledge or education can be reduced and classified as a wisdom question. A question about change, progress, or advancements can be reduced and classified as a technology question; a question about the majority's opinion or power of authority: community vs. individual; helping others to attain goals, giving up personal gain to accomplish a greater good: sacrifice; and so on.

The assignment presented in the first chapter ("Ease does not challenge us; adversity shows us who we really are.") is really a conflict question. Adversity refers to difficulty or challenges. You could write about a war, a battle with an illness—any struggle, any conflict.

Memorize the fifteen core topics!

Circle and define the key words within the essay assignment.

Here are some other recent SAT essay excerpts and assignments, all reduced to one of the fifteen core topics. Remember, focus on what the assignment is asking you, not the complexities of the excerpt.

The people we call heroes do not usually start out as unusual. Often, they are ordinary people subject to ordinary human weaknesses—fear, doubt, and self-interest. In fact, they live ordinary lives until they distinguish themselves by having to deal with an injustice or a difficult situation. Only then, when they must respond in thought and in action to extraordinary challenge, do people begin to know their strengths and weaknesses.

ASSIGNMENT: *"Do people learn who they are only when they are forced into action?"*

THEME: Heroism (There's also some overlap into a conflict essay.)

"A man with one watch knows what time it is; a man with two watches is never quite sure."

ASSIGNMENT: *"Does truth change depending on perspective?"*

THEME: Truth/perspective

Technology promises to make our lives easier, freeing up time for leisure pursuits. But the rapid pace of technological innovation and the split second processing capabilities of computers that can work virtually nonstop have made all of us feel rushed.

We have adopted the relentless pace of the very machines that were supposed to simplify our lives, with the result that, whether at work or play, people do not feel like their lives have changed for the better.

ASSIGNMENT: *"Do changes that make our lives easier necessarily make them better?"*

THEME: Technology/changes

Every time you read an essay assignment—SAT, English class, global studies, or otherwise—see whether you can relate this question to one of the fifteen core topics. The more you practice, the more second nature the process becomes, the more prepared you are on test day, and the more points you earn.

The SAT is not meant for those who like surprises: you now know exactly what's coming when you open that little booklet of fun on test day. But knowing what to expect is only half the battle. You've got to know what to write and how to write it if you want to win the war.

FIFTEEN CORE TOPICS REMINDER SHEET

The Core topics listed below are developed throughout the book. Memorize these core topics to be prepared on test day!

- Choices

- Competition vs. Cooperation

- Conflict

- Conscience/Ethics

- Creativity

- Group vs. Individual

- Happiness

- Heroism

- Motivation

- Perfection

- Perspective/Truth

- Sacrifice/Suffering

- Success

- Technology/Change

- Wisdom

"The loftier the building, the deeper must the foundation be laid."
THOMAS A KEMPIS, 14TH CENTURY PRIEST, MONK, AND WRITER

CHAPTER 3

LAY A FOUNDATION OF STAND-ALONE SENTENCES

Okay, kids—story time.

Once upon a time, there were three little pigs. They were all pretty fat and had outgrown their homes. So, each pig set out to build his own, more spacious house. One of the pigs just kicked some straw into a pile and jumped on in. Another one leaned some sticks together and created a mini-cabin. The third pig first found a nice piece of flat land, built himself a platform, and then constructed walls of brick, one at a time. Afterward, he went grocery shopping and did his laundry, as he is clearly a responsible pig. The rest is history—some big, bad wolf came by, blew the straw pile away and ate the first pig, kicked the sticks out of the way and ate the second pig, and gave up trying to eat the third pig—there was no huffing and puffing those brick walls down.

The moral of this story: Build a strong house.
The point of this story: An essay is like a house.

You are writing a persuasive essay. If there are weaknesses in the argument you construct, the reader will tear this argument apart. (Fortunately, he won't eat you. Unfortunately, he will give you a poor score.) So, in order to avoid your metaphorical house from being knocked down, you need to create a solid platform on which you will build your essay.

> Your thesis should summarize your essay's main point, direct the reader, and stand out like a blinking neon sign.

The Platform: A Thesis Sentence

As a high-school student, you know what a thesis is. It's your main idea, main point, answer to the question, etc. You must clearly state your thesis in your essay! This thesis is the platform you need to frame an appropriate response. If you have a weak thesis, it's like building a house on quicksand. You don't want quicksand. You want bedrock. This leads us to my next secret:

SECRET #3

CONSTRUCT A ROCK-SOLID, STAND-ALONE SENTENCE THAT ANSWERS THE ESSAY QUESTION AND SUMMARIZES YOUR ESSAY'S MAIN POINT.

The thesis sentence is the most important sentence in your essay, so make sure it is clearly stated and easy to spot. The thesis sentence most often belongs at the end of your introduction. Graders are looking for this thesis, and you don't want to make them look high and low! The faster the graders read, the faster the graders get paid; they don't want a scavenger hunt. Remember, you're building a house, not a secret hideout.

Constructing a bulletproof, reinforced, one-sentence answer to the essay question is easy. Just follow the simple formula: main idea + supporting example(s).

To understand the difference between a strong thesis sentence and a weak one, compare the following:

ASSIGNMENT: *"Are people motivated more by fame and money or by their conscience?"*

THESIS A: People are motivated by many things.

THESIS B: Famous football star Pat Tillman and German industrialist Oskar Schindler both show through their actions that people are motivated more by conscience than by money or fame.

ESSAY DIRECTION: Examples showing how Tillman and Schindler were motivated by their consciences rather than by money or fame.

The second sentence is, by far, the better thesis. It relates directly to the essay question and gives specific detail. This detail prepares the reader: the essay will be about Pat Tillman and Oskar Schindler and the ways in which both demonstrate that conscience is a powerful motivator. The first thesis sentence not only fails to definitively answer the essay assignment, but also in no way prepares the reader for what comes next.

Here are some more examples of strong thesis statements:

ASSIGNMENT: *"Are heroes ordinary people?"*

THESIS: Rosa Parks and Martin Luther were ordinary people who did extraordinary things, demonstrating that heroism is in all of us.

ESSAY DIRECTION: The extraordinary and heroic behavior of Rosa Parks and Martin Luther.

ASSIGNMENT: *"Should people always side with the majority?"*

THESIS: Through the actions of Gandhi and Martin Luther, we see that great minds don't always think alike and that people should not blindly follow the opinion of the majority.

ESSAY DIRECTION: The actions of Gandhi and Luther that went against the majority's opinion.

Every essay must have a stand-alone and easy-to-find thesis sentence.

A topic sentence couples the main idea with the direction that will be taken in the paragraph.

ASSIGNMENT: *"Does technology make the world a better place?"*

THESIS: Both global warming and the threat of nuclear war show that, contrary to what some believe, technology has only complicated and nearly destroyed the world as we know it.

ESSAY DIRECTION: Examples of negative technological effects.

🗝 Follow the thesis formula: *main idea + supporting example(s).*

Notice that the thesis sentence completely and wholly answers the essay assignment and gives specific and clear direction. Each thesis relies on the same formula: main idea + supporting example(s).

A thesis worksheet is included at the end of this book so that you can practice building your essay platform. Remember, your essay must include a well-constructed, stand-alone thesis statement.

CHECKLIST FOR EVALUATING THESIS SENTENCES

- Does the sentence answer the question?
- Does the thesis sentence introduce your main supporting points?
- Is the thesis sentence an overgeneralization? That is, does it make a statement too broad to prepare the reader for the details that follow?
- Do all the other topic sentences take their direction and focus from the thesis?

Once you've firmly established your building site and poured the concrete (yes, a thesis metaphor again), it's time to build your house. There is no way you can start with the furniture, the window treatments, or any other frilly little finishing touch that fills a home. These details are added after you've finished construction.

But how can you decide on what color wall paint, what size television, and what style stair railings you'll use in only twenty-five minutes? How will you plan the details of your house? Relax. Breathe. You'll know which details and decorations to include once you've framed in your space.

Topic sentences are the space-framing and defining walls of your essay. A topic sentence states the main idea of a paragraph and directs the sentences that follow. A good writer makes the topic of a paragraph immediately clear to the reader—hence topic sentence—and also guides the reader as to what comes next. In short, the topic sentence is a summary of the content of a paragraph.

Now, imagine you're writing an essay about heroism, and you want to write about Atticus Finch, the hero of *To Kill a Mockingbird*.

Take a look at the following topic sentence:

Atticus Finch from To Kill a Mockingbird is a main character.

Okay, so what? This is a poor topic sentence because it gives no direction. This topic sentence sets up a plot summary essay. Dull.

Kiss-of-death reminder: Do not put plot summaries in your essays! The graders on the SAT are well versed in literature. If you read the book in school, they'll know it, too. In fact, always assume that the reader has read the literature you're mentioning. Give at most a two-sentence overview of the book, and then move on to specific details.

Once again, do not develop a plot summary in your essay! A good essay encapsulates the heart of the book and provides the details to support a position—plot summary is not necessary! Creating a strong topic sentence that clearly presents the direction of the paragraph eliminates this plot summary construction.

… And I have to say it. There is no "making up" a book, either. Making up a book means you have to make up a plot and make up characters, and by the time you've developed a

Do not develop plot summaries in your essay. Rather, give a one- or two-sentence overview of the literature.

little fantasy story, you've wasted too much time and too much space on your paper!

So no, nein, nee, nay, na, non: You may not make up a book on the day of the test, in any language!

Back to topic sentences . . . . The first topic sentence about Atticus Finch was weak because it set up an essay that had to be a plot summary. Now, take a look at the second topic sentence below:

> Atticus, the protagonist in <u>To Kill a Mockingbird</u>, is a hero because he adheres to a strict moral code

Much better! Now we've set up guidelines. Atticus is a hero . . . the main idea of the paragraph. He is a hero because of his integrity . . . . Expand on this idea. The rest of the paragraph will include details and support expressing his integrity.

Notice that using the word "because" creates the effectiveness of this topic sentence. A simple method to create strong topic sentences is to use the formula: main idea + because + direction. This allows you as a writer to maintain focus; it also tells the reader what to expect. For more practice on topic sentences, complete the worksheet at the end of this book on p. 174.

Follow the thesis formula: *main idea + because + direction.*

Again, a comparison:

> 1. *Wisdom can be defined in many different ways.*
> 2. *George in <u>Of Mice and Men</u> defines wisdom because of the way he cares for Lennie.*

The first sentence gives me a main idea—that wisdom can be defined several ways. But I am given no direction. This sentence is not leading me, the reader, anywhere.

The second sentence is a much better topic sentence. A specific main idea is stated—that George defines wisdom in the way he cares for Lennie—and the reader is also told what to expect. The rest of the paragraph will be examples from *Of Mice and Men* that exemplify wisdom.

Let's say you were responding to the question "Is creativity needed in the world today?" (This question relates to the core topic creativity.) You plan to write about the Renaissance and the Scientific Revolution—eras of immense creativity. Your topic sentences should not only introduce each era, but also give the reader direction. Note the following examples:

During the Scientific Revolution, iconoclastic physicists, astronomers, and biologists challenged the established dogmas of science **because** *they took a more creative and inquisitive approach to studying natural phenomena.*

CORE TOPIC: Creativity
MAIN IDEA: Scientific Revolution emerged as an era of creativity
DIRECTION: The creative and inquisitive developments that challenged the established dogmas of science

This topic sentence prepares the reader for details about Galileo and the telescope, Copernicus and the heliocentric theory, or any other creative scientific advancement of the time.

Another example:

The Italian Renaissance illustrates the necessity of creativity and novel ideas **because** *the artists, philosophers and humanitarians of the time allowed for drastic advancements in art, science and philosophy.*

CORE TOPIC: Creativity
MAIN IDEA: The Renaissance shows that creativity is necessary
DIRECTION: The drastic advancements that resulted from creative thinking

This topic sentence prepares the reader for the details and specifics of the Renaissance. Once again, notice the basic formula: main idea + because + direction.

Remember, the SAT encourages formulaic writing. Knowing the formula is the key to success!

Topic sentences are like mini-thesis statements ("mini" because they apply to a paragraph rather than the whole essay). Topic sentences, then, like thesis statements, should be stand-alone sentences that clearly present an idea.

CHECKLIST FOR EVALUATING TOPIC SENTENCES

- Is the main idea presented by the topic sentence?
- Is the topic sentence an overgeneralization? (That is, does it make a statement too broad to be really useful in understanding the paragraph?)
- Do all the other sentences in the paragraph take their direction and focus from the topic sentence?

So, to summarize, be a smart pig. Build a good house by starting with a solid foundation and by constructing brick walls. And pssst . . . the secret: your house is resting on three strong, stand-alone sentences—a thesis and two topic sentences.

Of course you can elaborate and "flower up" your thesis and topic sentences as much as you'd like (not all houses have to look alike). But, the successful essay keeps everything simple. The simpler the formula, the easier to memorize. The easier to memorize, the easier to pre-write and repeat on test day.

Remember, the SAT essay is a standardized, formulaic, twenty-five-minute, on-the-spot essay, not a three-week, brainstormed, edited, peer-reviewed, submitted-for-a-prize English term paper. Even for these extensive English class assignments, for which you have the time to flower up, it's best to start with the basics and go from there.

Regardless of the fanciness level you attain, there are various structures of houses you can build. This structure depends on the examples you choose to include and the details you can provide, as explained in the next chapter.

"Style and structure are the essence of a book;
great ideas are hogwash."
VLADIMIR NABOKOV, RUSSIAN-AMERICAN NOVELIST

CHAPTER 4

KNOW THE TYPE OF HOUSE YOU'RE BUILDING

Now it's time to build the house—the essay itself—on your thesis platform. I realize you're a teenager and most likely don't have a degree in architecture. I also realize you probably haven't even set up a tent before, let alone built a house. Regardless, I'm confident that if you were you to build a house, you know you'd need a plan. And, you'd know the type of home you were building before you started nailing and sawing and constructing.

SECRET #4

KNOW THE TYPE OF HOUSE YOU WILL BE CONSTRUCTING BEFORE YOU BEGIN TO BUILD.

There are only three possible formats for writing the SAT essay. It is important to know each of these formats so that you can structure and develop a strong argument.

Know the three essay structures detailed in this chapter!

Remember, you only have twenty-five minutes. You have no time to waste figuring out how to build or organize. You want this organization to be second nature. Therefore, know and practice each structure before test day.

THE TRADITIONAL STRUCTURE

"The Classroom Essay"

Introduction
- define the quote in your own words
- agree or disagree with quote
- state thesis

Body Paragraph 1
- develop a specific supporting example

Body Paragraph 2
- develop another specific supporting idea

Conclusion
- restate the quote in your own words
- sum up evidence and knock down the opposition
- broaden your essay to the "now"

As you may notice from the above outline, this is the structure of a standard essay. It is also the most popular format on the SAT, and the essay structure with which you and other high-school students are most familiar. The traditional structure is the essay structure you've been trained to use in the classroom, and this training is a good thing. You already know how to effectively structure a traditional essay—one less thing to worry about on test day.

As you know, the traditional essay structure requires that you have a clearly stated thesis at the end of your introduction and that you include two supporting examples in two separate body paragraphs. These two separate body paragraphs must be linked, inseparably, by a strong transition.

Think of your essay as a flight of stairs. You should be able to step from the introduction to body paragraph one, and then from body paragraph one to body paragraph two, and then right to the conclusion. You don't want someone climbing through your essay, arriving at a giant hole, and freefalling to your conclusion. Trust me, graders do not want to freefall. They want an easy, smooth read. You give them that, and they'll give you a good score.

Note: Transitions are a crucial element of stylistic writing and are further detailed and exampled in Chapter 5.

Below is an example of a stellar* traditional essay written by a former student in response to the assignment: *"Does truth change depending on perspective?"*

*STELLAR
Outstanding

Who's right? Who's wrong? There isn't always a clear-cut answer to these questions, because as the old saying goes, "truth is relative." There are a myriad of literary and historical examples, including <u>To Kill a Mockingbird</u> *and French Algeria, demonstrating that truth is in the eye of the beholder.*

Set in racist Maycomb, Alabama, Harper Lee's <u>To Kill a Mockingbird</u> *shows two different truths from different perspectives. When Tom Robinson, a black man accused of raping Mayella Ewell, a white girl, was brought to trial, the townspeople were blinded by their bigotry and racism and refused to see the possibility of Tom's innocence. Despite the substantial amount of evidence that his lawyer, Atticus Finch, presented in Tom's defense, the people of the town could not and would not believe that Tom Robinson was innocent. For them, the truth was simple: Tom Robinson was guilty. The truth was also simple for Atticus Finch. A man of integrity, logic and justice, Atticus saw beyond the cloud of racism that enveloped the town. The truth, according to Atticus, was that Tom Robinson was innocent. Because of the angle the situation was looked at, there were two very distinct and very different truths seen.*

This same situation of seeing things from different perspectives is seen historically as well. During the 1940s,

The all-in-one essay is a traditionally structured essay that focuses on one example. Only use the all-in-one structure if you can bring up two distinct assertions and back these assertions with facts.

torturous acts in French Algeria were seen as justified and horrific depending on whom you asked. Algeria, a primarily Muslim country, was under French control. After WWII ended, the Algerians decided they wanted independence from France. The French military immediately tried to put down the rebellion that ensued, and it became quite bloody. The Algerian nationalists used terrorist tactics, which prompted the French government to take drastic measures. The French generals confessed that torture was used to gain information from the terrorists. In the mind of the French army, this was the only way to protect their people and preserve their colony. But the French people saw a different truth, that torture was unacceptable under any conditions. They saw the practice as not only a heinous act, but also a strike against France's honor. Once again, perspective changes the concept of truth.

Different viewpoints can change the truth for different people, as is clearly evident based on historical events and literature. Some argue that like in math and physics, there is only one absolute truth. However, even the laws of science change depending on conditions. Truth is relative to the perspective of the person who sees it.

The above essay addresses the core topic of truth/perspective. It uses the traditional structure to express two main supporting examples: *To Kill a Mockingbird* and French Algeria. Note the definitive thesis and strong topic sentences that summarize the main idea and outline the details to follow (Secret #3). Each distinct idea has its own distinct paragraph, but the paragraphs are linked by the transition: This same situation . . . .

The Traditional Essay . . . with a Twist

Sometimes, though, you might want to write a traditional essay that revolves around just one supporting example. For those of you who happen to be a guru in a certain area (maybe you know everything about Walt Disney's career or about every boxing great), you can write a traditionally structured essay that revolves solely around your area of expertise.

This "all-in-one" traditional essay only works if you are truly an expert on the subject and can include lots and lots of details. The all-in-one essay still follows the premise of the standard traditional essay. The introduction provides a clear thesis. The body paragraphs highlight two ideas, both relating to your area of expertise. And the conclusion sums everything up and restates the thesis.

Below is an example of an excellent all-in-one essay in response to the assignment: *"Does enduring a situation or acting against a situation make a person courageous?"*

By the way, the core topic for this one is heroism (with some conflict overlap). The topic sentence is bold.

Courage. Courage is the power to fight for what one believes in, and to continue fighting no matter how difficult or dangerous the fight may be. **The Abolitionists of the Civil War era showed tremendous courage in their efforts to free Southern slaves because they acted against the institute of slavery by developing the Underground Railroad and by acting as a driving force behind the Reconstruction era.**

In the time period leading up to the Civil War, the institution of slavery in the South reached new levels of cruelty that Abolitionists stood up against. Northerners took extreme measures in order to end the cruel institution, helping to form the Underground Railroad. This was a secret, dangerous pathway that led slaves from the South towards freedom in Canada. The Abolitionists and slaves alike risked capture, imprisonment and even death—but never gave up. Harriet Tubman, an escaped slave, Union spy and avid Abolitionist, risked her life to save over 70 slaves. Abolitionists, like Harriet Tubman, proved they were courageous on many levels in their persistent fight to end slavery.

The Abolitionists did not end their courageous fight against slavery after the Civil War had ended. From 1861 to 1865, many bloody battles were fought, and ultimately the North won the war. The slaves were freed indefinitely, but many felt that their lives worsened: The KKK formed; oppressive Black codes were enforced, and ex-slaves were left homeless and jobless. The former Abolitionists refocused their efforts and aided newly freed slaves in building homes and finding jobs. Frederick Douglass, one of the leading voices for equal rights, convinced President Grant to outlaw the KKK and helped lead to the arrest of thousands of Klan members. All of this was done under tremendous oppression and violent opposition.

The Abolitionists refused to surrender until their goals were met. Although lives were lost, families were divided, years of turmoil, riots and violence ensued, the Abolitionists found the courage to fight for what they believed in. Many people argue that the Abolitionists were law-breaking rebels, but the Abolitionists' efforts to end slavery demonstrated strength and intrepidness.* To be courageous is to prove that one is willing to fight no matter what the consequences may be. Today, we see this same principle in our troops who risk their lives in order to protect their country and provide a better future for the people of both Afghanistan and the United States.

*INTREPIDNESS
Fearlessness

This entire essay revolves around the Civil War, with each body paragraph focusing on one specific aspect. The first paragraph provides the background of the situation; the next addresses the Underground Railroad; the last details the Abolitionists' efforts during Reconstruction. This student had two distinct assertions relating to a single topic and backed each of these assertions with details and specifics. Again, the all-in-one essay is at heart a traditional essay. Keep that in mind when structuring your response.

Often students ask, "How do I know which example to use first and which example to use second?" My answer: If you're writing about one topic, such as the previous Civil War essay, it's best to write in chronological order. If you're writing a standard traditional essay, it's best to use your strongest example last. This is what a grader reads right before he scores your essay, so save the best for last!

The traditional essay is the classic style and structure used to present information in a logical, coherent manner. However, there will be some cases in which you won't be able to come up with two strong supporting, or one truly in-depth example. Don't panic! If you can't build your house in the traditional manner, you can build it in a not-so-traditional manner.

Rule of Thumb: for the traditional essay, save your best example for last.

THE SANDWICH STRUCTURE

Introduction
• begin with a specific example
• use example to define thesis in last sentence

Body Paragraph 1
• develop a second example to support thesis
• relate this example to the original example

Note: This essay requires a strong transition linking the original example with the second example.

Conclusion
• restate thesis
• re-examine the first example

The sandwich. Bread … bologna … bread. (I do realize a bologna sandwich is not a house, but a sandwich is eaten in a house, so work with me!)

The sandwich essay involves two distinct ideas, with the big, meaty, juicy, detailed idea in the middle. The sandwich essay is created by beginning with one idea, moving on to a well-supported and developed second idea, and then coming back to the original idea at the end of your essay.

This structure is good for several reasons. First, you only need one fully developed example: the meat in the middle. Second, it starts with a detail (and the SAT loves detail) that immediately grabs the reader's attention. Third, the sandwich structure allows you to weave a formal tone with an informal tone: for example, you can put your detailed example in between a personal narrative. And last, the sandwich structure is different. "Different" means you'll steer clear of mediocrity.

But be careful! This essay, like the traditional essay, only works with strong transitions. Without transitional sentences, this essay becomes more of a sloppy joe than a sandwich. If you're talking about Grandma in the first paragraph and Shakespearean characters in the next, and then jump back to dear old Granny, the reader can easily get lost.

A few good transitions to completely change ideas (and that are absolutely necessary in a sandwich-structured essay):

• *On a personal note* . . . (transition into personal example)
• *On a much smaller scale* . . . (transition from historical to current/personal event)
• *A similar, yet fictional, person/concept is depicted in* . . . (transition from real life to literature)

> Note: A more comprehensive list of useful transitions is included at the end of Chapter 5.

The beauty of the sandwich structure is that you are giving the reader something unexpected. Almost every SAT taker begins with an introduction that rewords or reworks the quote in a boring paraphrase. Sandwich-style writing incorporates a strong detail into the introduction so that the beginning of your essay starts out on a more powerful and different note than everyone else's. But, you must remember to use this detail to lead the reader into your thesis.

Just like the traditionally structured essay, the sandwich essay requires that your thesis sentence is the last sentence of the introductory paragraph.

To give you a better understanding of how the sandwich essay works, below is a former student's essay, written sandwich-style, in response to: *"Are people motivated more by fame, money, and power, or do people find personal fulfillment more rewarding?"*

"I am going!" I said to my mother. The summer was fast approaching and I had finally made up my mind. But the truth was that I didn't want to go. I was dreading saying goodbye to my home for three weeks—I had never been away for more than three days at a time! My mother kept telling me that I didn't have to go away to camp; that the world would not end if I chose to stay home. But my mother didn't understand. I had to go. I had to go and prove to myself that I could be away from my parents and my close circle of friends, where I felt in control. I knew that if I went away for those three weeks, I would gain a sense of personal satisfaction.

Like myself, there are others who do things not to gain celebrity but to gain a sense of personal fulfillment. Pat Tillman is one such person, motivated by his conscience, not fame and fortune. Pat Tillman had wealth and recognition as a football star. People perceived him as happy—a man who had it all—but they were wrong. Just before the football season began, Pat Tillman shocked the nation when the media leaked that he had decided to enlist in the U.S. Army and would not continue his football career. After hearing about the situation in Afghanistan, Tillman had enlisted in the army quietly and didn't intend to make his decision a public one. When asked, Pat said his motivation for joining the military was just something he knew he had to do. He didn't want fame or wealth; he wanted to gain personal fulfillment. That is what drove him to military service and sadly, to his untimely death soon thereafter.

Although a small feat compared to Tillman's, I left for camp that summer. Saying goodbye to my parents and friends was the hardest thing I've ever done. However, after that goodbye I made it through the three weeks just fine, with the exception of a few cuts and bruises. I wish I could say it was the best summer of my life, but it wasn't. I wasn't popular, I wasn't the best water skier, and I left with only a few new friends. However, when I got home, I was different. The immense happiness I felt from successfully completing my first summer away from mom and dad gave me new confidence. I felt better, more independent, and stronger. This feeling was in itself the best reward I have ever gotten.

Notice that Pat Tillman is the main, detailed example of this essay. This example is stuck between a less detailed personal narrative. The reader is thrown immediately into this narrative, transitioned out, and then transitioned back in at the end. The transitions "Like myself" and "Although" are crucial to this essay.

Both the traditional- and sandwich-essay structures require that you have some supporting examples drawn from outside knowledge. But what happens if you freeze on test day? What happens if you can't think of a single thing to write about? Well, my friend, in that case, you write about you and a build a completely non-traditional house: a narrative essay.

THE NARRATIVE STRUCTURE

Intro/Body Paragraph

• create an anecdote that responds to the essay question

• begin "in the moment" with a story

• develop story and anecdote

Conclusion

• rework the essay assignment in the form of a thesis.

• state how your story proves or disproves the essay assignment

This last structure—the narrative—is the "outside-the-SAT-box" structure. It is a completely nontraditional response. However, don't be afraid to use this structure. If used properly, the narrative format can be very powerful, very thought provoking, and thus very high scoring. I want to stress, though, that you must follow the provided formula for the narrative to be effective.

The narrative essay involves the use of a personal story to exemplify the meaning of the assignment. You must make sure that your personal story illustrates your position and addresses the complexities of the question.

This format calls for descriptive writing, dialogue, humor, concrete examples, active verbs, and figurative language (Secret #5). Show, don't tell. Your essay needs to essentially paint a picture for the reader: be sure to provide lots of concrete, juicy details. Open your essay "in the moment" by starting in the midst of something. And then really hit home at the end by restating the essay assignment in the form of a thesis.

For example: *It was an early Wednesday morning when I received a call from the Montclair Volunteer Ambulance Unit.* This is an excellent opening sentence because it immediately envelops the reader in the narrative. From here, build the story toward your main point: the thesis. This is the one structure

Use detailed personal examples in the narrative structure if you don't have any historical, literary, or current-event examples to write about. Don't be afraid to make something up!

in which the thesis is not found in the introductory paragraph but is stated in the last paragraph. Even though you're not stating your thesis until the end of the essay, make sure it is implied throughout.

Your entire essay is a story—a story about you. At the end of this story, you need to assertively answer the essay assignment by directly applying your narrative to the prompt. Qualify your broad and abstract ideas with explicit details so that what applies to you personally can be applied elsewhere. Readers must understand your situation, so make it clear to them through detail and concrete references. To do this, end your essay with the direct SAT quotation. So in your essay: *story, story, story . . . and that is why "people's lives are the result of the choices they make."*

Below is a superb essay written in the narrative format in response to this very question: *"Are people's lives the result of the choices they make?"*

"Don't Americans think we're stupid? We feel that they have no respect for us." I was stunned. It was Thursday evening, and I was teaching a Hispanic man English through a volunteer program. My friend and I taught regularly, but we had found it frustrating and sometimes boring. However, this night completely changed my perspective. Our students excelled at English and surprised us with their knowledge. We focused on their colloquial English, and ended up talking for the entire two hours of class.

During this time, we were able to get to know them and see our language and culture from their perspective. They pointed out the difficult irregularities in English grammar and shared their thoughts on our culture. What caught me off guard was the impression that they thought most Americans had of Hispanics. They said that they feel Americans are condescending and disrespectful towards

> The thesis is found in the conclusion of the narrative essay. End the narrative by restating the essay assignment.

Hispanics and Hispanic culture in general. What they said has been on my mind ever since . . .

Despite their impressions of most Americans, the two men thanked my friend and I for our assistance and willingness to help without belittling them. This is when I realized that "people's lives are a result of the choices they make." Many people don't take the opportunity to befriend someone from a different culture. One of the men asked if I would tell my friends about our conversation. I intend to pass this message on, because I want to make choices that will benefit others' lives. By choosing to teach English to others and seeing things from someone else's viewpoint, I have enriched my life, as well as the lives of others. What I used to think of as a burdensome job has shown me a new perspective. "People's lives are the result of the choices they make." I choose to help others, and as a result, my life is rewarding.

Notice that the thesis statement is stated clearly at the very end of the essay, and that it is taken directly from the SAT question. This is what really "hits home" in a narrative essay.

Realize that the SAT is testing your writing ability—not your ability to recall facts. Therefore, if you're stuck on test day and can't think of examples, make something up! Make up a story about your mother or your best friend. (They love you unconditionally so it doesn't matter what you say about them in your essay!) Be creative—make up a personal anecdote and stuff it with juicy details! Although you're embracing your creative license, try not to write about a pivotal sports moment or an experience in junior high. Those stories tend to be a bit cliché. Rather, try writing a narrative about a family crisis or a vacation you took.

On test day, you'll have to decide which essay structure to use based on the examples you will be writing about. Remember, there is no building a house without a set plan!

When writing a narrative essay, follow the strict formula: begin with an anecdote, develop this anecdote through illustrative writing, and then relate this anecdote to the essay assignment.

If you have two distinct and substantial examples, build a traditionally structured essay. If you have one substantial example and a slightly weaker second example, utilize the sandwich structure. And, if you can't seem to brainstorm any examples or if you happen to have a terrific (and relevant!) anecdote to share, write a narrative. Don't be afraid to make up details!

STRUCTURE RECAP

Use this sheet to refresh your memory on how to build a powerful essay in three different ways.

THE TRADITIONAL STRUCTURE (Use if you have two distinct and substantial examples.)

Introduction
• define quote in own words
• agree or disagree with quote
• create thesis

Body Paragraph 1
• develop specific supporting example

Body Paragraph 2
• develop another specific supporting example

Conclusion
• restate the quote in your own words
• sum up evidence and knock down the opposition
• broaden your essay to the "now"

THE SANDWICH STRUCTURE (Use if you have a substantial example and a weaker second.)

Introduction
• begin with a specific example
• use example to define thesis

Body Paragraph 1
• develop a second example to support thesis
• relate this example to the original example
  Note: This essay requires a strong transition linking the original example with the second example.

Conclusion
• restate thesis
• re-examine the first example

THE NARRATIVE STRUCTURE (Use if you have no examples or a great anecdote to share.)

Intro/Body Paragraph(s)
• create an anecdote that responds to the essay question
• begin "in the moment" with a story
• develop story and anecdote

Conclusion
• end with direct quotation of essay question
• state how your story proves or disproves quote

"Don't tell me that the moon is shining; show me the glint of light on broken glass."
ANTON CHEKHOV, RUSSIAN AUTHOR/PLAYWRIGHT

CHAPTER 5

ENTICE THE READER WITH STYLE

You know the patterns, you know how to build a foundation, and you even know how to structure an essay. But you're hesitant. That first sentence seems so difficult to write . . . .

Tick, tock. Twenty-five minutes leave no time for writer's block. You need an opening sentence that strongly starts off your essay; you need an opening sentence that engages the reader; you need an opening sentence with some flair! But how? It's simple: include five basic but essential elements of style within your essay. These elements add the needed pizzazz that will keep a reader interested and, more important, persuade the reader that your position is correct. However, the limited (very limited) time frame of the SAT often saps the creativity out of an essay and makes the essay dry and conventional, AKA boring. If you practice writing with style and make these elements second nature, you will transform the boring into the compelling.

The above paragraph showcases each of the five essential elements of style:

1. **Sentence variety:** Tick, tock.
2. **Thought-provoking questions:** But how?
3. **Repetition:** You need . . . you need . . . you need.
4. **Transitions:** However . . .
5. **Active word choice:** will transform boring into compelling.

Now, I'm a professional (and a show-off!). Although I've included each element of style in a single paragraph, you do not have to. Nor should you. Not only would this be time consuming, but it would also cloud the message. In a persuasive essay, a clear and convincing message is crucial to a high score. The secret is to deliberately insert *some* rather than drown your essay with these five style points.

SECRET #5

ENTICE THE READER WITH STYLE AND WOW THE READER WITH THE FIRST SENTENCE.

Know the five elements of style and make these elements second nature.

Imagine 120 essays all about the same topic (this is the standard number of essays each grader reads). What is going to make your essay stand out from the others? A little style, that's what. If your essay does not differentiate from the other essays, you will not be able to achieve a top score of 9-12. Including the stylistic elements detailed in this chapter ensures that your essay shines!

I know, I know. There are only twenty-five minutes. There's no time to make your writing "pretty." And you're right. Which is why you're going to practice and make style a part of your normal routine. Just like putting on make-up or getting rid of that five-o'clock shadow is a part of your daily "spruce up," stylistic writing should become a part of your regular writing habits, too. Follow the simple formulas below to make style-rich writing part of your routine. Not only will this sort of writing attain a top SAT score, but it will also help you get that A+ in Mrs. Smith's third-period English class.

Element 1: Vary Sentence Lengths

Sentence variety is truly the key to preventing readers from falling asleep. If every sentence has the same structure—boring! Writing without sentence variety is like talking in a monotone. And you definitely do not want your essay sounding monotonous.

Look at the following paragraphs. The first is written without varying the sentences; the second uses sentence variety.

ASSIGNMENT: *"Are flaws more interesting than perfection?"*

WITHOUT SENTENCE VARIETY:

Models and movie stars are envied. They are envied because they are perfect. They are beautiful and they are glamorous. They are envied by the average Jane and Joe because on TV they look perfect. They are projected to be perfect though, and they are not really perfect. Perfection does not exist. Everyone has interesting flaws.

Ugh! Almost every sentence is the same length and begins with "they." And this is just an introduction. Imagine a whole essay written just as uniformly! Again, ugh!

WITH SENTENCE VARIETY:

Models. Movie stars. Glamorous people on TV, in magazines, and living a lavish life in Hollywood are envied by the average Joe and Jane. It is easy and understandable to envy the celebrities and models seen on television and in movies; they are aesthetically* perfect. Flawless faces, long legs, unblemished skin—who wouldn't want to look absolutely perfect? But perfection is unobtainable and does not exist. These glamorous movie stars are only projected to be perfect. Each one is littered with various flaws that the average Jane and Joe don't see on television. I too am littered with flaws, and I don't have them airbrushed out. Flaws are what make me . . . me.

*AESTHETICALLY
Pleasing in appearance

Ahhh . . . much better. Notice how the same point is being made, but the introduction is written with much more variety: a one-word sentence (fragment) followed by a simple sentence and then a compound-complex sentence. Not only does the

Limit fragments to one per essay.

paragraph sound less boring, but it also sounds sophisticated—and sophistication will get you a higher score on the SAT. Also, although you've been told never to start with a fragment, you've been lied to. When used correctly, starting with a fragment can be very powerful. However, your essay should only contain one fragment. Otherwise, you lose the effect and appear to have no idea what a "true" sentence really is.

By the way, this paragraph also includes a thought-provoking question—bonus points! Read on . . .

Element 2: Add Thought-provoking Questions

Adding engaging and thought-provoking questions is a great way to add a "bang" to your introduction and body paragraphs and to push your essay to the next level—to above average. The following two SAT essay responses demonstrate how thought-provoking questions can be used to effectively enhance your writing.

ASSIGNMENT: *"Do changes that make our lives easier necessarily make them better?"*
CORE TOPIC: technology/changes

The Industrial Revolution—quite possibly the most exciting period of American history! Technology advanced at an incredible rate. It seemed that everyday innovative ideas were manifested; Americans witnessed invention after invention, from the refrigerator to the telephone. Life was becoming more and more convenient. But where were these inventions being manufactured? Factories and sweatshops. These places of manufacture represent the darker side of the Industrial Revolution, run by cutthroat Robber Barons. Thus, the Industrial Revolution created a wretchedness of life for Americans of that era.

The questioning in this introduction is fantastic. It introduces a specific example of fast change and decreasing quality of life that leads the reader to the thesis.

Another example . . .

ASSIGNMENT: *"Can average people accomplish heroic feats?"*

What makes a hero? Is it a cape and mask? Is it the power of X-ray vision? To be heroic people do not need to exist in the realm of comic books. Heroes are those who embrace integrity, courage, and empathy.

The questions are found smack in the beginning of the essay. Wow! Already the essay has me thinking, mentally answering the questions I have just read. Notice that the writer answers the questions he poses. You, too, should answer any questions that you pose in your essay. This way the reader can't come up with the "wrong answer." Remember, you're proving your point—don't leave any room for second-guessing! Note, though, that an essay should not contain more than three questions. Too many questions turn your essay into a philosophical-sounding monster!

The three questions above also established repetition, the third element of style . . . .

Include no more than three thought-provoking questions per essay.

Element 3: Use Repetition to Your Advantage

Your writing should be logical, balanced, and parallel if you want to leave an impact on your audience. Repetition helps create this impact by selectively emphasizing certain ideas and by establishing continuity.

However, be careful not to be so repetitive in your writing that you lose sentence variety. Remember, you are deliberately using *some* of these elements in your essay for maximum effect.

Below are some examples that exhibit good repetitive writing.

Pick a key word/ phrase to repeat for emphasis and impact.

ASSIGNMENT: *"Should those who are most experienced or those who are most prepared be considered wise?"*

Wise individuals know the answers to most questions; wise individuals know how to help others; wise individuals know how to take action and take control of a situation. As one can see, there are many different definitions of wisdom. But, the most important definition of wisdom is experience.

ASSIGNMENT: *"Is it more important to consider the rights and goals of the group or the individual?"*

The right to bear arms, the right to free speech, and the right to a fair trial—the rights of the individual must always trump the rights of a community.

The SAT essay is partially graded on length. Bring in several ideas and connect these ideas with transitions.

Notice that in both of these cases, a short phrase is repeated within a sentence to emphasize the point being made. Repetition does not involve structuring every sentence in an essay the same way. Nor does repetition boil down to creating "shopping lists." Effective repetition involves repeated, parallel words, phrases, or sentence structures, not repeated items. The idea is to strategically pick a key word/phrase to repeat for emphasis: make your point by constructing repeating, parallel phrases. This technique is used to make a powerful impact on the audience—think State of the Union address, presidential speeches, debates, etc.

Element 4: Use Strong Transitions

High-school students often struggle with transitional phrases. As discussed in Chapter 3, transitions are crucial within all essay structures. They are the sentences that link different ideas and make your writing flow so that a reader can swim through a paragraph and move to the next one. There should be no abrupt changes in topic.

Transitions are also crucial in circulating writing around a central point. When used effectively, transitional phrases allow a writer to illustrate the main idea with several different examples. This is important because the SAT essay is graded on length. Write two full pages! It's difficult to write two pages in twenty-five minutes on just one idea. Thus, you will be writing about several ideas and will need several transitions.

Below is an example of effective transitional phrases used between body paragraphs. They are bolded.

ASSIGNMENT: *"Do you think that ease does not challenge us and that we need adversity to help us discover who we really are?"*

Gandhi. Martin Luther King, Jr. George Washington. These men were faced with countless challenges and difficulties that led to their success and greatness. Gandhi's stand against the English involved long, toilsome protests. Martin Luther King Jr.'s oppression and battle for equality ultimately led to his assassination. George Washington's bloody revolutionary battles gained him the prestige and honor of becoming the first American president. Despite all odds against them, they rose to the occasion, enduring and overcoming adversity.

***On a personal note**, I too have faced great adversity and fought what seemed to be a losing battle. My mother was diagnosed with breast cancer three years ago and I was certain that my family would be torn apart and she would die. The chemotherapy did not seem to have any effect on the cancer; my father had to pick up extra shifts at work to pay for medical treatments; I could not bear the sight of my dying mother and avoided being with her as much as possible. I reasoned with myself that the situation was too emotionally burdensome for any teenage student, that no one could expect me to act any differently. For the* *first month my mother was in the hospital I only visited once.*

However, my avoidance of the situation did not ease my or my mother's suffering and I realized that I needed to give strength to my mother if she was to fight this cancer. I found myself smiling, laughing and telling my mother it would be okay, regardless of the fear and terror I felt inside. And when she won the battle and came home from the hospital, she hugged me and whispered, "You pulled me through." My mother will always be my mother, and I will always be her daughter. But in a time of desperation, fear, and chaos, I found it in me to take care of her.

This essay begins with cliché historical examples that are used to grab the reader's attention. However, these examples are addressed only briefly, before leading the reader to the main focus of the essay, the author's mother. The flip from history to her mom, though, is done gracefully, with aplomb* because of the transitional phrase, *On a personal note.*

*APLOMB
Poise

Rather than just jumping from one idea to the next, this phrase greases the runway. The reader can smoothly and quickly shift gears and prepare for a topic shift. Then the essay switches topics again. The daughter avoided the situation for a month, and then realized that this was not a good idea. The writer doesn't toss the reader from negative feelings to positive feelings. Rather, the writer again prepares the reader to shift gears by transitioning with *However.* Even though ideas and topics are switching, everything centers around the main point: *adversity makes us who we are.*

Remember: As you write, keep the main idea in focus. Persuasive transitions prepare and guide the reader and also keep the reader focused on your main idea.

The following is a list of easy transitions that allow for a graceful change of topic between body paragraphs. Memorize these transitions!

On a personal note . . . (switching to personal experience)

More recently . . . (switching from history to present)

This is also seen in . . . (a general switch)

More realistically . . . (switching from literature to history/ personal)

I had a similar experience . . . (general switch to personal)

Just as X, Y also demonstrates . . . (a general switch)

At the end of this chapter you'll find a more complete list of transitional phrases. Memorizing several of these transitional phrases will bring you that much closer to a pre-written essay—Secret #1!

Element 5: Establish Active Voice

When writing, be aggressive. Don't just scribble your ideas down on paper—slap the reader in the face with them. Thoughts are very powerful when you use an active voice to express them. Both active and passive forms of verbs get the message across, but the passive voice yips like a miniature poodle while the active voice barks like a German shepherd. Bark! A reader is much more affected when they are barked at by large-dog active verbs.

> *Active "large-dog" verbs create intensity and often appeal to the senses.*

The following are some examples comparing active and passive verb forms. **P** represents the passive form; **A** represents the active form.

P *Jim was hit by Jack.*

A *Jack hit Jim.*

P *A note is being written by Emily.*

A *Emily is writing a note.*

P *The ball was hit by Andy's left foot; even so, a goal was scored by him.*

A *Andy hit the ball with his left foot; even so, he scored a goal.*

Notice how the passive forms just breeze by. *Jim was hit by Jack.* Oh, okay. That's nice. *Jack hit Jim.* Bam! Whoa, Jack's violent; he's hitting; Jim's hurt. I'm affected by this sentence now. I'm engaged as a reader.

Persuade the reader with active verb forms.

Also, remember that deep down your SAT essay is a persuasive essay. You want to present your ideas as facts. By using the active voice to engage the reader, your essay will be more persuasive.

Using the Five Elements of Style to Your Advantage

The five elements of style are really what make a good essay good. Writing with style makes for sophisticated writing, and sophisticated writing will help get you those 100 extra points. Once again, the secret is to use the five elements of style to lure the reader; to grab the reader's attention and to keep the reader's attention until the very last sentence.

HOOK: BEGIN WITH A BANG

Begin with a bang! Open with a captivating sentence.

Plan on starting your essay with one of the five elements of style—begin with a bang! You want to punch the reader in the face. Bam! Here's my essay! Wake up! My essay is terrific, so pay attention! Starting with sentence variety, repetitive structuring, or thought-provoking questions is the way to punch the reader and begin with a bang.

Take a look at the following sentence:

I agree with the quote that it is adversity that motivates us.

Never put "I agree" in your essay.

This sentence bores me. First of all, *never* put "I agree," "I believe," or "I think" in any essay—whether it is this twenty-five-minute SAT essay or an essay you are writing for English class. Obviously you agree, believe, or think what you're writing—it is your essay!

Even if your beginning sentence reads something like, *It is true that adversity motivates us*, I am still bored! This is a standard sentence. You don't want standard, you want persuasive; you want different; you want enticing!

Now, look at the following sentences:

Adversity. One little word that changed my life.
(SENTENCE VARIETY)

It was a summer of intense heat; it was a summer of long days; but most of all it was the summer that would change my life. **(REPETITION)**

Why is it that bad events often shape who we become? **(THOUGHT-PROVOKING QUESTION THAT DIRECTLY ADDRESSES THE PROMPT)**

These sentences are powerful. They add a punch that makes the reader want to keep reading. The goal of the introduction of the twenty-five-minute essay is to not only address the question, but also to make the reader want to read on.

Once again, let me reiterate. Unless you punch the reader at the beginning, you have a very good shot of only getting a score of 8 or below. You must impress the reader from the beginning to score a 9 or above.

Know the five elements of style: sentence variety, thought-provoking questions, transitions, repetition, and active voice.

Having been an essay grader and a high-school English teacher, I know that the introduction is the key to a strong grade. Immediately, a qualified teacher/grader/SAT essay reader can tell if the essay is going to stand out from the pack or be the same old answer. Adding the elements of style to an opening sentence, especially the opening sentence of a traditionally structured essay, will hook the reader.

You already know what to expect—an assignment that can be reduced to one of the fifteen core topics. Once you have your core topic, simply plug it in to one of my simple but effective template "hooks." These guarantee the *punch*.

Note the formulas for and examples of these three template openings that include a hook and a thesis statement. All examples are written in response to the following assignment: *"Are heroes born great or are they ordinary people who do great things?"*

Hook 1: Repetition

The *topic* is X, the *topic* is Y, but most important, the *topic* is Z.

A hero is strong, a hero is courageous, but most important, a hero demonstrates integrity.

Hook 2: Sentence Variety

One-word sentence. Definition.

Heroes. Heroes are ordinary people who risk their safety to help others.

Hook 3: Thought-provoking Question

Take the theme and highlight the concept in a question.

What does a person have to do to become a hero? A person needs to make the right decision in a time of difficulty.

Memorize these hook formulas so that come test day, you won't waste time or break a sweat due to writer's block. You'll know exactly how to begin a powerful and terrific essay. Simply choose whichever hook you'd like and plug in the core topic. For practice, complete the worksheets included at the end of the book.

Show; don't tell. Use descriptive, concrete writing.

Show, Don't Tell

Adding the elements of style to your introduction is crucial to engage the reader from the start. But it is equally important to keep the reader engaged throughout. Showing, not telling, does just that. You've heard "show, don't tell" since first grade, but what does it mean for the SAT essay?

In each body paragraph, make sure you're showing your point, not just telling it: Use lots of detail to entice and persuade the reader to see and understand the issue from your point of view. Be specific. Remember the senses—smell, sound, sight, touch, and taste. Appeal to emotions! Impact the grader! Through stylistic and concrete detail, you're metaphorically waving a steak at a bear. The grader will take the bait and eat up every word of your delicious writing.

Take a look at the following paragraphs taken from a narrative-structure essay. The second is re-written for punch and power and is clearly more enticing. Remember, in a narrative essay you're proving your point through a personal anecdote. It is especially important that you write with detail and flair, so that your story really addresses the question thoughtfully and thoroughly and leads the reader where you want him to go.

ASSIGNMENT: *"Is it true that man unites himself with the world through creativity?"*
VERSION 1: Standard.

This first paragraph is written in a subjective format, bringing in "I." However, the persona, as written, is boring and nondescript and fails to leave an impression on the reader.

> *Throughout high school, I have excelled in advanced math and science courses. I have also been very successful in my art and design courses as well. This is why I plan on being an architect. I experience a tremendous amount of enthusiasm when I have the chance to create something and build things on my own. Even from the time I was a child, I always loved to draw and create things of my own. I feel that in my near future, I would love to be involved in the arts in some capacity . . . .*

VERSION 2: With pizzazz!

This version is written more abstractly, but the message is made clear through vivid and emotional appeal, as well as concrete, descriptive sentences.

> *A twelve-pack of Crayola markers was never enough for me. I needed the markers that changed colors when you put water on them, that disappeared when you drew over them, that had different shaped tips that made unique*

designs. I was a child that spent hours with a pad and a few hundred markers in front of me; I loved to create.

I remember the excitement I felt in my seventh-grade home economics class when the teacher told us we would be making corn muffins in school starting from scratch. To be able to add ingredients such as flour, sugar, eggs, etc., and end up with an edible muffin thrilled me to no end. I couldn't wait to go home and try it myself. Cooking provided me another outlet for creation.

Notice how, as a reader, you're drawn into the second version and are able to picture the narrator. The writer has *shown* you, rather than just *told* you, about the value of creativity in his life.

Here's another example:

ASSIGNMENT: *"Is it better to be just a 'face in the crowd' or to stand apart?"*
VERSION 1: Standard.

I am hoping that my strong sense of being a unique individual will bring me success in life. I enjoy taking risks. I enjoy "leading the pack." Being involved with numerous people increases my desire to make an impact in some way on what's going on around me. I believe that my will to achieve perfection along with my organizational skills will allow me to be a highly accomplished person in the near future. My sensitive and emotional attitude towards others will allow me to be a pertinent individual to society.

VERSION 2: With pizzazz!

A gun was pointed at my sister's head. The shooter held the piece straight to her ear. "Through one side and out the other," I thought. Her lips began to quiver. Her big blue eyes filled with tears. Her skin tone took on a ghastly complexion. Right as the gunman held onto my sister's skull, bracing for impact, my sister broke into pure hysteria. The gunman lowered the weapon. Now was my chance. After the metal pierced my skin, I realized the power one feels when making a significant decision or taking a major risk. Having an earring at the mere age of eight was an empowering symbol that I chose to exhibit. Perhaps it is this mindset that I have that differentiates me from everyone else.

I drive a yellow Jeep Wrangler; I wear Converse high-tops; I sport Ray Ban Aviators. I enjoy being a person known for adding the extra twist of creativity; for putting the icing on the cake.

Notice the difference between the standard writing that talks about vague generalities and writing that deliberately chooses specific words and images that engage and guide the reader to experience and understand the topic from the writer's point of view. The examples provided were all narrative vignettes—mini-narratives that can be used effectively to suck readers into a story as it leads them toward a concrete thesis.

Beginning with a narrative vignette can be an effective way of hooking the reader, as long as you're careful not to ramble on for too long. If you are planning on continuing with a full, detailed narrative, make sure you follow the formula for this essay structure. Another way to show rather than tell in a narrative essay is to use dialogue. Opening with dialogue grabs the reader and throws them headfirst into your personal anecdote.

Open the narrative essay with dialogue to immediately involve the reader.

TO SUMMARIZE, YOUR ESSAY *MUST* INCLUDE:

- sentence variety
- thought-provoking questions
- active voice
- repetition
- transitions

AND JUST AS THERE ARE *MUSTS*, THERE ARE *MUST NOTS*:

- Don't write vague general statements. Be concrete and specific!
- Don't create "shopping lists" that string ideas together without emphasizing anything.
- Don't catalogue with ho-hum generalities.

REMEMBER, YOUR GOAL IS TO *SHOW*, NOT *TELL*.

So, on the day of the test, be strong, be dynamite, and give 'em a bang in the introduction! Start off with a carefully chosen hook. Vary your sentences. Use repetitive phrasing judiciously. Make your voice active and engaging. Ask thought-provoking questions. In other words, write with style throughout your essay so that your writing is engaging, descriptive, and powerful from the very first word to the very last period.

TRANSITIONAL PHRASES

Transitions move a reader from one topic to the next. Memorize the lists below.

To introduce a new detail . . .

As evidence

For example

For instance

In fact

In support of this

To support an opinion . . .

Also

Besides

Equally important

First/Second/Third/Finally

Further

Furthermore

In addition

Likewise

Moreover

Similarly

Concluding phrases . . .

As noted

As you can see

For the reasons above

In conclusion

In other words

In short

In summation

On the whole

To be sure

To sum up

Unquestionably

To qualify (alter) an opinion . . .

Although

Besides

But

However

Nevertheless

Nonetheless

On the contrary

On the other hand

Yet

Moving to history . . .

(Theme) has been seen throughout history

If we look to our past, we see (theme) as well

More realistically (switching from literature)

Moving to current events . . .

This same problem is confronted today in society

Modern times also reveal (theme)

More recently

Moving to personal . . .

I had a similar experience

On a much smaller scale, I experienced (theme)

I was confronted with the very same problem

"Advice to young writers: Don't write about man, write about a man."
E.B. WHITE, AMERICAN WRITER

CHAPTER 6

PICK NOW; WRITE LATER

So let's say you're going for the traditional or sandwich-structured essay. You already know to begin your essay with a bang and to state your thesis clearly. You have some idea about the style elements you'll want to use. But what goes after the introduction and before the conclusion? How will you develop, detail, and substantiate the main part of the essay?

Given twenty-five minutes, many students who do not know the secrets of writing the SAT essay right will only have enough time to lay down two slices of bread, slap on some greasy mayonnaise, and bon appétit—a weak sandwich (or traditional) essay!

Would you order this sandwich from the menu? Absolutely not! It's missing the meat—the delicious detail that a reader craves! (Detail is crucial to every essay structure. Your essay—whatever the format may be—needs to be jam-packed with these details.)

I know, twenty-five minutes! How can you possibly beef up your essay with detail? Easy—be prepared! The next few chapters will help you pre-select examples and specifics from history, literature, current events, sports, and your personal experiences to include in your essay.

Pre-selected examples and details will allow you to pre-write your essay (Secret #1). You want to pre-*everything*. Remember, all of the work and preparation (*pre*-paration) should be done

Pre-select your examples and details so that you can pre-write your essay.

before you arrive on test day. This "pre-" guarantees that above-average score.

PRE-SELECT YOUR SUPPORTING EXAMPLES AND MEMORIZE FIVE FACTS ABOUT EACH.

The next few chapters will help you choose examples from literature, history, current events, sports, and your personal experiences that can be used to support your essay's position.

Bear in mind that the reader craves details and interesting facts. Superficial statements and vague generalities are just plain boring to read. Pre-selecting examples will help turn an average essay into a persuasive monster of an essay because you will be able to include lots of persuasive details and pertinent* facts. Therefore, the secret is to pre-select examples from each category and memorize five concrete details about each one. On test day, choose which of your pre-selected examples best apply to the essay assignment.

*PERTINENT
Relevant

Own Three (Interesting!) Historical Moments

"No harm's done to history by making it something someone would want to read."

DAVID MCCULLOUGH, AMERICAN AUTHOR

I have read literally thousands of SAT essays, and I know that many students do mention examples from history. However, they do just that—they *mention* history. In twenty-five minutes, the average student has difficulty coming up with the details necessary to really support their essay; therefore, they only bring in a cursory,* mundane* examples without adding any juicy details.

Good thing you're no longer the average SAT essay writer. You're becoming the above-average writer: the student who

Pre-select your examples and memorize five facts about each.

*CURSORY
Superficial
*MUNDANE
Boring

will grab extra points on the SAT because of above-average essay preparation.

Specifics, concrete details, and facts are going to elevate your essay to this above-average essay. The goal is to memorize and include concrete examples and interesting facts (and, if possible, even a date) for three historical moments.

Take a look at this weak historical detail included in response to the following assignment: *"Can success be disastrous?"*

> *During the Civil War, the North was competing with the South, and the North succeeded, freeing the slaves but leaving some people unhappy.*

What is this proving? Everyone knows that slavery was abolished. This is a superficial, boring account of the Civil War, exactly the type of account that will prevent you from reaching a top score on the SAT essay. And "some people unhappy"? This is another superficial statement that gives less-than-clear direction.

As a grader, I need concrete examples! Beef up your essay with battles, dates, names, places, etc. If you are going to use a historical example, you need to own that example. You should be able to give a history lesson about that example! Know your examples inside and out, backward and forward, "in a box, with a fox, in the rain, and on a train"—own your examples!

> *From 1861 to 1865, the northern and southern United States entered into a period of bloody civil war; although the North's success emancipated slaves, the country was thrown into a period of economic and social instability.*

Oooh—much more interesting. I have a date, I have a place, and I have a direction as to where the essay will be going: how the North's victory was both successful and disastrous. This sentence allows the writer to bring in details of the Reconstruction Era (period after the Civil War). These are new details—about the birth of the KKK, tax increases for the South, the oppressive Black Codes, and the assassination of Abraham Lincoln.

Remember, you can't write a full paragraph without several concrete details. Otherwise, you'll end up repeating that the North won and the South lost. Everyone knows this! Thus, know a handful of details and facts about your historical moments.

Own three historical moments.

Now, regardless of how much of a history buff you consider yourself, you can't be an expert on all historical events. Choose three, and own these three. ("Owning," again, means knowing inside and out. Nothing superficial!)

There are thousands of years of recorded events to choose from, so select wisely. As interesting as the cavemen and the slaying of the woolly mammoth may be to you, this period in history does not relate to many of the core essay topics.

Rather, choose topics that address several of the core essay topics—re-read your history book, Google search your topic, study an encyclopedia, and own your topics! (Let's be honest: it's less time-consuming to use the Internet—that's what I recommend.)

The Internet is a valuable resource for getting quick facts!

I also recommend that your historical moments include one war, one era, and one historical figure. These should be disparate moments in history so that you cover all of the core topics. Don't choose the Civil War, the Civil War Era, and Abe Lincoln. Those are all the same details and relate to exactly the same core topics!

A little note: Technology is a difficult core topic to address through history. However, it can be easily addressed through current events, detailed later.

The following is a list of some good historical moments to own. Feel free to pick three of these moments or to come up with some of your own. But choose wisely—go back and look at the fifteen core topics. Think about which historical moments easily relate to several of these core topics. You want to be doing as little work as possible! Remember to choose one war, one era, and one historical figure.

Also, just a reminder, the Holocaust, Martin Luther King, Jr., and September 11 do relate to a majority of the core topics. However, these examples are overused, and overused is average. Instead, try writing about Oskar Schindler, Malcolm X, or Darfur, examples that still relate to a majority of the core topics but that are less used and more interesting.

Wars:

Darfur

The American Revolution

The Barbarian Invasion/Fall of Rome

The Civil War

The French Revolution

World War I

Eras:

Cold War Era

Enlightenment

Immigration

Industrial Revolution

Scientific Revolution

Women's Suffrage Movement

Figures:

Ben Franklin

Charles Darwin

Galileo Galilei

Gregor Mendel

Malcolm X

Martin Luther

Nelson Mandela

Oskar Schindler

Presidents: FDR, Washington, Lincoln, Jefferson

Rosa Parks

Thomas Edison

Wright Brothers

Choose three historical moments to own: one war, one era, and one historical figure.

Do not write about the Holocaust, Martin Luther King, Jr., or September 11.

Remember you want real, interesting, specific, juicy details—not boring overview statements or vague and superficial generalities. You don't need to read your 800-pound American history textbook to find these details, either. Just take three minutes online, and jot down five interesting facts.

Be aware that interesting does not mean random! Random facts will cause you to lose the focus in your essay. If you find yourself describing what sort of moustache a certain general had during the Civil War, you're off track. You need to relate your examples and details back to your thesis and the definitions of your key words. Moustache styles won't relate!

The following are two charts outlining Abraham Lincoln. The first chart contains absolutely useless "moustache details." The second chart contains specific and *relevant* details that relate to the various core topics.

Superficial/Random Details

Lincoln was the first president who was assassinated.

In 1840, Lincoln became engaged to Mary Todd. The couple split as the wedding approached.

Only one of Lincoln's children survived to adulthood.

Lincoln almost drowned in Knob Creek but was saved by a neighbor boy.

Relevant/Specific Details

One of the most successful presidents of the United States, Lincoln knew how to reunite the country and keep morale up in the Union during the Civil War.

Issued the Emancipation Proclamation in 1863 to start liberating slaves.

He used his knowledge and presidential power to keep the border slave states on the Union side.

Lincoln delivered his iconic speech, the Gettysburg Address, and asserted that it was the nation's duty to give a "new birth of freedom."

John Wilkes Booth assassinated Lincoln.

Notice that the details in the first chart do not relate to the core topics and offer no substantial information about Lincoln. Make sure your details can be used to provide support in your essay!

Notice also that the second list provides an overview of Lincoln's accomplishments, details several salient* facts about his presidency, and explains the ending point of Lincoln's presidential era. If you are detailing an era or a war, you would want to note the causes of the conflict or origins of the era, include several key events, and how/when/why the era or conflict ended.

Finally, I want to emphasize that you should really only own three moments. If you consider yourself an expert in everything, you're probably an expert in nothing. So fewer examples, more details!

The following model historical chart illustrates how to organize the details that you will memorize. You can use the template on p. 186 to create your own chart.

*SALIENT
Of notable significance

MODEL HISTORICAL MOMENTS CHART

Figure	Applicable Core Topics
Name: Nelson Mandela Dates: 1948-present	Conflict Conscience Group/Individual Heroism Motivation Sacrifice Wisdom

Facts	
1. The leading figure against the apartheid beginning in the year 1948 2. He opened the first black legal firm in South Africa. 3. He was influenced by Mahatma Gandhi but went against Gandhi's principle of nonviolent protest as a last resort effort to end apartheid. 4. He was inaugurated as the first democratically elected state president of South Africa in 1994. 5. In 2009, the United Nations General Assembly announced that Mandela's birthday is to be known as Mandela Day to mark his contribution to world freedom.	

Era	Applicable Core Topics
Name: Women's Rights Movement Dates: 1820s-1900s	Competition Conflict Group/Individual Happiness Heroism Motivation Sacrifice

Facts	
1. Began with the writings of Fanny Wright and led to the Seneca Falls convention 2. Women gained support after the Civil War because they were angry that black men had been given the right to vote. 3. Susan B. Anthony, Elizabeth Stanton, and Frederick Douglass were leading proponents. 4. "Frontier" states such as Wyoming and Colorado granted women the right to vote in hopes of attracting more female settlers. 5. The United States finally granted women the right to vote in all elections in 1920 with the 19th Amendment.	

War	Applicable Core Topics
Name: Thirty Years War Dates: 1618-1648	Choices Conflict Group/Individual Heroism Motivation Sacrifice

Facts
1. Many political and religious causes led up to the war, including competition for land and the development of Calvinism. 2. Protestants in the Holy Roman Empire revolted against the new Catholic emperor. 3. Many European countries helped one of the religious groups, depending on which religion was predominant in their own country. 4. All of Europe was involved: this war was one of the most destructive wars in European history. 5. "Peace of Westphalia" resolved the conflict; all three religious groups (Protestant, Reformed, Catholic) were defined as equal and each country was able to choose its own religion.

Own Two Literary Works

"There are two motives for reading a book: one, that you enjoy it; the other, that you can boast about it."

BERTRAND RUSSELL, BRITISH PHILOSOPHER/MATHEMATICIAN

*COPIOUS
Plentiful

Literature, like history, offers copious* examples that may be used as support in an essay. Choose two pieces of literature to own. Slip the books under your pillow and read them before the test. Study SparkNotes. Recite passages to your friends in the school cafeteria. Know the characters, know the plots, know the themes, and know the quotations. Own them!

Pull out a couple of key quotes from the literature that relate to a core topic.

Once again, be smart in your selection. Although R.L. Stein's *Goosebumps* collection may be your favorite series and you've read the books every day from sixth grade on, *Goosebumps* aren't quite considered classic pieces of literature that offer timeless themes. And ladies, neither are steamy romance novels—sorry! Shakespeare's *Romeo and Juliet*, *Macbeth*, and *Hamlet*; Harper Lee's *To Kill a Mockingbird*; and Steinbeck's *Of Mice and Men* are some excellent works that offer rich, supportive details that revolve around many of the fifteen core topics. Choose two of these pieces or different pieces of equal merit to own for test day.

On test day, try to bring one—and only one—of your two literary examples into your essay. Graders like students to bring in a variety of support, not just literature. At the end of this chapter, you'll find a list of excellent literary works to use for a twenty-five-minute essay.

Know two pieces of literature inside and out.

As a former English teacher, I recognize that the SAT generally relies on classic literature such as Harper Lee's *To Kill a Mockingbird* and John Steinbeck's *Of Mice and Men*. I might be a bookworm and happen to have many of these literary works at my fingertips. However, because you are students, I only expect you to know two works of literature. I've provided a bulleted plot summary of both *To Kill a Mockingbird* and *Of Mice and Men*. You should create a similar, bulleted plot summary for the work you choose. I've also included a chart that highlights some specific examples from each book. Blank charts are provided for you to organize your own literary details around the fifteen core topics.

Remember that the Internet is a valuable resource. Save time: SparkNotes. CliffsNotes. Google. Although re-reading your book of choice is best, reviewing the books online is a good way to brush up.

Do not use more than one literary work per essay.

PLOT SUMMARY FOR *TO KILL A MOCKINGBIRD* BY HARPER LEE

- A coming of age story about Scout Finch and her brother Jem
- Takes place in fictional town of Maycomb, Alabama
- As the story unfolds, the children learn about prejudice and that the world is not always a kind place; life does not treat everyone equally.
- Jem and Scout befriend a boy named Dill, a boy who stays with his aunt in the summer.
- The three children are terrified and fascinated by their neighbor, the reclusive Boo Radley.
- Boo sparks their imagination because he is never seen and never comes outside.
- Scout learns about the inequalities within her community by attending school.
- Walter Cunningham does not have food to eat, and Scout invites him for dinner.
- Burris Ewell frightens Scout, and Burris ends up dropping out of school.
- One summer, the children find that someone is leaving them small gifts in a tree.
- Atticus is appointed by the court to defend Tom Robinson, a black man who has been accused of raping Mayella Ewell.
- Atticus agrees to defend Tom Robinson even though the community objects.
- Atticus stands watch at the jail and faces a group of men intent on lynching Tom.
- Scout, Jem, and Dill shame the mob into dispersing.
- Scout shames the mob by recognizing Walter Cunningham's father and singling him out in the crowd.
- The children watch the trial from the black section—upstairs in the courthouse.
- Atticus establishes that the accusers are lying.
- Despite significant evidence of Tom's innocence, the jury convicts him.
- Tom, knowing he will never be a free man, escapes from prison and is shot and killed.
- Humiliated by the trial, Bob Ewell vows revenge.
- Bob Ewell spits in Atticus's face, menaces Tom Robinson's widow, and attacks Jem.
- Boo Radley saves Jem from Bob Ewell and Jem's arm is broken in the fight.
- The sheriff decides to "protect" Boo Radley by stating that Bob Ewell died because he fell on his own knife.
- Scout walks Boo back home.
- While standing on Boo's porch, Scout imagines life from Boo's perspective and regrets that they never repaid him for the gifts he had given them.

CHART FOR *TO KILL A MOCKINGBIRD*

Useful Quotes
1. "It's a sin to kill a mockingbird." -Atticus Finch
2. "Atticus was right. One time he said you never really know a man until you stand in his shoes and walk around in them." -Scout Finch
3. "The one thing that doesn't abide by majority rule is a person's conscience." -Atticus Finch

Core Topic	Relative Details
Choices	1. Boo Radley decides to come out of his home to save Jem. 2. Mrs. Dubose decides to die "clean" and morphine free.
Competition/ Cooperation	1. Mrs. Dubose decides to compete at the end and to die clean from her addiction. 2. Atticus chooses to fight a losing battle—the Tom Robinson case. He knows that fighting for Tom is the right thing to do.
Conflict	1. Atticus vs. town 2. Nathan vs. Boo
Conscience/ Ethics	1. Atticus is motivated by his conscience. 2. Sheriff is motivated by his conscience to lie and break the law
Creativity	1. Atticus's defense of Tom Robinson and the evidence he presents 2. The antics of the children and their imaginations
Group/ Individual	1. Black community vs. white community 2. Atticus vs. the town of Maycomb
Happiness	1. Dill's friendship with the children 2. The children's relationship with Calpurnia and the close-knit black community
Heroism	1. Calpurnia (often overlooked as a hero) acted as a stand-in mother and instilled strong values and morals in Jem and Scout. 2. Atticus, because he refuses to sacrifice his integrity and fights against the injustices of racism
Motivation	1. Atticus and Mrs. Dubose are both motivated by personal integrity and conscience. 2. Boo Radley is motivated to come out of his home to save Jem.
Perfection	1. Telling the story from Scout's perspective as a six-year-old expresses how children are born "perfect" and racism and prejudices are learned rather than innate.
Perspective/ Truth	1. Bob Ewell is found innocent, but he commits the true crime, while Tom Robinson is found guilty. 2. Boo Radley is seen as a "monster" but is really a kind person who saves Jem at the end.
Sacrifice	1. Boo Radley sacrifices his privacy and comes out of hiding to save Jem. 2. Mrs. Dubose sacrifices her health and endures a lot of pain to die drug free.
Success	1. Mrs. Dubose successfully kicks her addiction and dies drug-free. 2. Atticus proves Ewell is guilty even though Tom Robinson is found guilty.
Wisdom	1. Atticus because of his penetrating intelligence and exemplary behavior 2. Jem exhibits wisdom when he cries that the hole has been filled in the tree because he understands the moral lessons of his father.

PLOT SUMMARY FOR *OF MICE AND MEN* BY JOHN STEINBECK

- Takes place during the Great Depression
- George Milton is an intelligent and cynical man, and Lennie Small is a huge man of immense strength but limited mental abilities.
- Both are friends and go to a ranch in Soledad, California (Soledad means "loneliness" in Spanish).
- They are fleeing from their previous job where Lennie was accused of attempted rape for touching a young woman's dress.
- George and Lennie have a dream of settling down on their own piece of land and raising rabbits.
- Lennie is unhappy at the new ranch until Slim, the head ranch hand, gives Lennie one of his new pups.
- At the ranch, the friends' dream begins to seem possible.
- Candy, an old, one-handed ranch hand, even offers to put up his savings so the three of them can buy a farm. Candy's dog dies, and Slim tells Candy that he should have put the dog out of his misery ages ago.
- Crooks, the black stable hand, also joins this group, hoping for a better life in the future.
- Curley, the ranch owner's son, enters the bunkhouse looking for his wife. He picks a fight with Lennie, and Lennie crushes his hand.
- By accident Lennie kills the pup that he had hid in his pocket.
- Curley's wife finds the distraught Lennie and offers to have Lennie pet her hair.
- Lennie inevitably becomes too rough, and accidentally breaks Curley's wife's neck.
- Seeing what he has done to the pup and Curley's wife, Lennie retreats to the secret place in the brush where only George will find him.
- Curley, a jealous and insecure man, determines to get revenge by assembling a lynch mob.
- George realizes that Lennie will get caught.
- In a final act of kindness, wanting to spare Lennie from the violent mob, George shoots Lennie in the back of the head.
- As George prepares to kill Lennie, he tells him for one last time about their dream of owning their own land.

CHART FOR *OF MICE AND MEN*

Useful Quotes
1. "I ought to of shot that dog myself . . . ." -Candy
2. "You hadda George, I swear you hadda." -Slim
3. "We kinda look after each other." -George

Core Topic	Relative Details
Choices	1. George's choice to kill Lennie 2. Candy's feelings about the decision to kill the dog
Competition/ Cooperation	1. Survival of the fittest—Lennie is "not fit." Lennie must die at the end according to Social Darwinism. 2. Lennie doesn't understand Curley and his jealous/inferiority complex.
Conflict	1. Curly's resentment and jealousy toward Lennie 2. George's conflict with Lennie
Conscience/ Ethics	1. The treatment of Crooks and Curly as well as George's decision to stick by Lennie all these years
Creativity	1. The dream of the rabbit farm
Group/ Individual	1. George and Lennie create their own community of friendship. 2. Crooks longs to be a part of a community, but racism prevents him from doing so. He is ostracized and lives with the animals.
Heroism	1. George stands by Lennie throughout the novel and makes the hard decision at the end to kill Lennie and save him persecution. A hero must have the courage to stand by his decision. George must live with the pain and guilt of killing Lennie for the rest of his life. 2. George—hero in the way he is accepting and tolerant of others' weaknesses; takes in Lennie, Candy, and Crooks. George has a strong sense of humanity.
Motivation	1. Candy and Crook's desire to be part of Lennie and George's dream 2. Curley's resentment and jealousy toward Lennie motivates his behavior.
Perfection	1. Man is flawed—Lennie, Candy, Crooks, and Curley all exhibit different flaws. 2. The perfection of happiness that is found within George and Lennie's friendship
Perspective/ Truth	1. George's killing of Lennie can be seen as cruel or as the ultimate sacrifice. 2. Slim's perspective of Candy and Curley
Sacrifice	1. George shoots Lennie for the good of society. 2. Curley sacrifices his dog for the community.
Wisdom	Slim: Men look to him for guidance. He is at "peace" with himself and understands the bond of friendship between Lennie and George. George is wise in his effort to protect Lennie; he understands men's hearts (understands Curley, Curley's wife, and he trusts Slim).

LITERATURE TO KNOW

The following is a list of excellent literary works that can be used to develop a strong, persuasive essay in relation to many of the core topics. Remember, you only need to be familiar with one or two of these pieces, not all of them!

- *Animal Farm* by George Orwell

- *Frankenstein* by Mary Shelley

- *Hamlet* by William Shakespeare

- *Lord of the Flies* by William Golding

- *Macbeth* by William Shakespeare

- *Night* by Elie Wiesel

- *Of Mice and Men* by John Steinbeck

- *Romeo and Juliet* by William Shakespeare

- *The Bluest Eye* by Toni Morrison

- *The Crucible* by Arthur Miller

- *The Great Gatsby* by F. Scott Fitzgerald

- *The Scarlet Letter* by Nathaniel Hawthorne

- *To Kill a Mockingbird* by Harper Lee

Own Three Current Events

"The art of life is to live in the present moment."
EMMET FOX, AUTHOR/LECTURER

History, literature, sports, and personal examples all provide powerful examples to support your thesis. But current events are an added bonus! Not only are current events easy to fit into most essays, but they will knock the socks off the grader. Writing about current political, economic, or environmental issues—the so-called "grown-up problems"—immediately catches the reader's attention.

Imagine:
"Hey, Mom. I know that greenhouse gases are making summer hotter and hotter and that your electric bill is getting bigger and bigger. I started a community service group at school that will go and plant trees along the canal. Also, I looked into those electric hybrid cars—you should check out this website."

After Mom has finished gawking and can speak again, she will clearly double your allowance and cook your favorite meal. Discussing current events in your essay leaves the same impression on a grader, only rather than Mom's homemade meatloaf, you'll get an above-average essay grade!

The current event details are easy to prepare for, easy to remember, and—because most students do not bring current events into their essay—gives you an easy way to make your essay completely original. By following the three simple steps below, you'll be able to effectively incorporate "the now" into your essay.

Comb through the *U.S. News* and *World Report, Newsweek,* and *Time Magazine* for feature articles that relate to the core topics.

STEP 1:

Two weeks (or even months before if you happen to see a good magazine while checking out of the grocery store) before the exam, pick up a copy of *U.S. News and World Report, Newsweek,* and *Time Magazine.* Every May, *Time* puts out the "100 Most Influential People" issue. Get it! (Your friends may call you a nerd, but you can laugh later when you get accepted into your first-choice school.)

STEP 2:

*PERUSE
Examine

Notice the covers—does the cover story relate to any of the fifteen core topics? Peruse* the magazines looking for feature stories that relate to the fifteen core topics. Are heroes being discussed? Global-warming issues? War feature stories? Recent deaths of famous people? Sports stars in trouble? Find three or four good stories (ones that relate to a handful of the fifteen core topics).

Remember your audience, though. Writing about Britney Spears or the latest celebrity gossip will not persuasively influence the readers as much as the current financial or business crisis. You're trying to persuade a middle-aged grader, not a tween.

> Relate a current event to the core topic to impress the grader.

Know the details of these stories—the names, the facts, the magazine you got the article from, and the month it was published. Own your moments!

STEP 3:

Below are a few current events—milestone happenings that fit nicely into a lot of SAT essays. Study the following list and know a few of the selected or pick your own. Use the Internet. Google. Yahoo. Wikipedia. Get online and get some interesting tidbits about what is going on in the world around you. Know three current events well (from the list below or from your own magazine searches)!

> Use the Internet to find interesting tidbits about the world around you and bring these into an essay.

Climate Change: HOT TOPIC! (Cheesy pun intended.) Human impact on the environment has swung into focus lately. Pollution, deforestation, overpopulation . . . yikes! However, people are tackling these problems: hybrid cars, recycling, plants, natural habitat conservation. All of these are great things to bring into a creativity or technology essay. But mentioning the greenhouse effect won't get you those extra points. Get online and get some good, concrete facts.

Oprah: Who doesn't love Oprah?! Oprah struggled through life when she was younger, but boy, did she ever make it big! And now she gives, gives, and gives. Oprah can fit into a lot of essays.

Barack Obama: During the 2008 presidential election, the country voted in its first African American president. Obama won a landslide victory. This election can be seen as a unifying event that demonstrates tolerance and progress.

Natural Disasters: Natural catastrophes, however devastating, unite the global community and prompt the world to help those in need. Consider including the tsunami in Indonesia, hurricane Katrina, the 2010 earthquake in Haiti, or another natural disaster in an essay.

Darfur: When the world became aware of the horrific mass genocide taking place in Africa, outraged voices could be heard everywhere. Just like natural disasters, genocide is a large-scale catastrophe (even more so as people are causing the destruction) that unites the global community, in this case, against moral injustice.

Beginning or ending with a current event can be very powerful. *Can be*. Don't just dump current events into a paragraph out of the blue without letting the grader know they are coming! No surprises = better grade. To introduce a current event, you must use a transitional sentence. Below are some simple but strong transitions to segue into your current events. Once again, memorize transitions!

POWERFUL CURRENT-EVENT TRANSITIONS

• Last year/month/week, I read an article in _____ about _____ that still resonates with me today.
• When we look at the world today we see _____.
• Current events depict this quote beautifully. Just look at _____.
• On a more current note, we see _____.

On the following page is a fantastic essay in the all-in-one traditional format about a "current" event (this one was written about the Martha Stewart financial scandal and subsequent insider trading conviction in 2004) in response to the question: *"Do memories hinder or help people in their effort to learn from the past and succeed in the present?"*

"Thinner, wealthier, and ready for Prime Time!" These were the powerful phrases that Newsweek magazine used to describe Martha Stewart after she was released from prison. Stewart is a businesswoman who engaged in fraudulent activities; however, her determination to correct the negative impacts of her actions on her career is leading her back to success.

After being accused of insider trading, Stewart denied having any sort of knowledge about the company whose stock she sold just one day before its value plummeted. But after weeks of investigation, it was determined that Stewart did indeed have knowledge about the company. In fact, she was very close to the executives of the company, and telephone records indicated that she had received a phone call from one of these executives just shortly before selling. A guilty Stewart was ridiculed across the country. Her company's stock began a downward spiral, and a movie mocking Stewart was put into production. With less money, a prison sentence, and a bad reputation, Stewart's future was far from promising.

However, Stewart learned from her mistakes, and she turned her life around. Instead of appealing her case to a higher court, Stewart accepted her prison sentence and the consequences of her actions. America responded supportively and enthusiastically to Stewart's display of integrity. As a result, her company once again became a billion-dollar enterprise and TV producers such as Mark Burnett negotiated a reality TV show.

Stewart's run-in with the law could have demolished her company and ultimately ruined her life. But her decision to willingly go to jail and make up for her actions has inspired millions of Americans whose support has made her career flourish once again. The memories of shame and imprisonment only motivated Stewart to better herself: she learned from her past mistakes and jettisoned herself towards future success.

This writer was obviously into baking and sewing, as she followed every aspect of Martha Stewart's career. But, maybe you're not so into modern business. Not to worry! The nice thing about current events is that they can be used to create fully developed essays, paragraphs, or be used as the "sugar on top" of your essay. Including just a sentence or two in the introduction or conclusion is enough to let the grader know you're aware of the world around you!

Use the chart on the following page to organize the current event details you'll have at your fingertips—and number-two pencil tips—on test day.

Other Details: Sports and Personal

> *"Sports do not build character. They reveal it."*
> JOHN WOODEN, AMERICAN BASKETBALL COACH

So you're a huge hockey fan, wear a foam-finger around the house, and don't miss a single broadcasted game—then by all means, write about a hockey player! Include an athlete in your essay!

Sports offer numerous examples of determination, success competition, failure, leadership, heroes, and more, all of which relate to the fifteen core topics. Be careful, though. It's not enough to mention football or baseball in general. You must mention specific sports moments or athletes to really prove your point. If you are going to include sports in your essay, you develop the example as you would literary or historical examples and provide concrete details, dates, and specifics.

There are incredible athletes who have overcome incredible obstacles, possessed extraordinary talent, or who serve as

Do not be afraid to write about a sports figure.

inspirational role models. Know the specifics of these athletes' careers, and include them in a well-developed, persuasive body paragraph.

Lance Armstrong: Overcoming all odds, Lance Armstrong beat cancer multiple times, all while remaining a top competitive athlete. Regardless of his medical conditions or doctors' advice, he competed in the Tour de France—and won! He's an example of success, competition, heroism . . . . He fits almost every essay topic!

Babe Ruth: Arguably the iconic face of baseball, Babe Ruth is regarded as one the best baseball players of all time, if not the best. He would fit into a perfection essay or hero essay, as well as competition (he "hit it big" once he was traded to the NY Yankees).

Pat Tillman: Professional football player turned Army soldier, Pat Tillman gave up his multimillion-dollar sports contract to join the military and fight in Iraq. He died in friendly fire, but as a true hero, one who sacrificed everything for what he believed in. He is a great example to include in hero, sacrifice, community, and conscience essays.

Michael Jordan: The ultimate example of "practice makes perfect," Michael Jordan used to shoot and make 100 baskets a day when he was younger. He is a great example of dedication, commitment, rising to the occasion, and perfection.

Fallen Athletes: Tonya Harding, Michael Vick, Barry Bonds, Tiger Woods . . . . Sometimes the money and popularity of being a star athlete becomes too much to handle and athletes fall off the right "track." Their stories continue, though. They may just make a comeback and be applicable to suffering, heroism, or wisdom essays.

Once again, only include sports if you're a sports junkie! If you don't know the difference between baseball and racquetball, have no idea what *15/Love* means, and get dizzy thinking of watching people run around a track, don't include sports in your essay! If you are planning to know sports details for test day, organize your examples and details in the chart provided on p. 193.

When You Become the Writing Topic: Personal Examples

Don't be afraid to include yourself within the essay, as your personal experiences may relate specifically to the core topics. Plus, you already know your personal life inside and out, so there is very little prep work involved! However, you must remember that by and large, high-school students have the same experiences. Limit your writing about game-winning soccer goals, the dream of making it pro, or that rival softball team. These tend to be very cliché. Equally cliché are the stories about the lunch table you used to sit at or the best friend you lost touch with.

Try writing instead about a vacation with your family, a particular argument with your mother, the death of a loved one, or a life-changing experience. Be specific! You must clearly illustrate your story with vivid details, illustrative language, and concrete details. It must also support the thesis of your essay and relate to the core topic.

For example:

VAGUE, GENERIC SENTENCE:

I once took a photograph that earned me recognition in my high school.

From an essay about . . .

CONCRETE, DETAILED SENTENCE:

"Gosh Rachel, what is that?" my friend Beth asked me. Suddenly, a crowd of students from my photography class was huddled around my latest photo. My face turned a deep shade of crimson.

From an essay about . . .

For a single personal experience, follow the narrative essay structure.

If you choose to revolve your entire essay around a single personal experience, follow the narrative structure. This structure involves beginning in the moment and ending the essay with a direct quotation of the essay assignment, which becomes your thesis sentence. Review this structure in Chapter 4. Also, I've included a chart to organize the pivotal moments of your life on p. 194.

"You were born to win, but to be a winner, you must plan to win."
ZIG ZIGLAR, AMERICAN AUTHOR

CHAPTER 7

PLAN YOUR ATTACK

Okay, you're armed with the secret of pre-paration, from knowing the fifteen core topics to pre-selecting and owning your key examples. You're now in the know about including specifics, details, and look-like-a-genius facts. And you're prepared to write about them with color and style.

But don't get carried away. As excited as you may be about including all the details you've memorized (after researching, organizing, and charting, I would be, too!), you need to hold back. Do not pour everything you know into your essay. This overflow waters down your essay and makes it less convincing.

Once again, the examples you use to support your position in your essay can come from literature, history, current events, sports, and your personal experience. However, you only have twenty-five minutes to write. You will not have time to fully develop examples from each area. Remember, traditional and sandwich essays each develop two supporting examples. On test day, you must decide which of the several examples you have prepared best addresses the essay assignment.

You must choose wisely on test day: you want to present your most convincing examples. There's no time for "eenie, meenie, miney, moe" in twenty-five minutes, though. Instead, take one or two minutes to outline the body of your essay and organize your argument.

> Do not try to include all your pre-selected examples in your essay.

You must outline and organize your essay's body paragraphs *before* you begin writing. Presenting the examples that best address the assignment and defining your thesis are essential if you are to truly persuade the reader.

So let's fast forward. It's test day. Your body is crammed awkwardly into a tiny, uncomfortable desk. The temperature in the room is set to either "Arctic blast" or "boiling lava," and, of course, you're seated next to a heavy breather. You open your test booklet. The assignment: *"Does one need to be highly competitive in order to succeed?"*

Your fellow test takers begin scratching their pencils simultaneously, writing feverishly. But your pencil marches to its own beat. You aren't diving blindly into your essay response because you're prepared. Your essay is not going to be disorganized and random like their essays. Your essay is (due to a two-minute outline) going to be logical and coherent. Your essay is going to be terrific!

SECRET #7

DO NOT START WRITING UNTIL YOU'VE OUTLINED YOUR SUPPORTING BODY EXAMPLES.

Outline and organize *before* you write a single word.

There are lots of outlines: formal outlines, bulleted outlines, outlines with Roman numerals and lowercase letters, outlines of your hand that can be made into turkeys ... but you are aiming for a simple, one-minute outline, one that will organize the body of your essay and help to determine which essay structure to use.

So, on test day, before you jump on the pencil-scratching bandwagon, follow these four steps:

STEP 1: CIRCLE THE KEY WORDS

The moment you read the essay prompt, pinpoint the key words in the question. Use these key words to relate the assignment to one of the core topics. We've already talked about key words in Chapter 2.

STEP 2: DEFINE THE KEY WORDS

The key words in the hypothetical test-day situation I described (*"Does one need to be highly competitive in order to succeed?"*) are "competitive" and "succeed." If you do not define these vague/abstract terms in your introduction, you will not do well on this essay. What one person views as success (being healthy throughout life, perhaps) is different from what another person views as success (maybe gaining enormous wealth). It makes no difference how you define the key words, but your essay should be designed to show that your definitions are correct. Remember, you are writing a persuasive essay. If you choose to define success as health and longevity, be sure to provide the grader with examples of health and longevity that result from competition.

STEP 3: OUTLINE POTENTIAL EXAMPLES

Your supporting body paragraph examples are pulled from literature, current events, history, personal experience, and sports. This is a broad spectrum, and on Section 1 of the four-hour test, your brain might be acting like a scrambled egg. So, here's a cutesy little way of remembering the various areas from which you've pre-selected examples: **L**-ittle **C**-hildren **H**-ave **P**-lay **S**-ets (L, C, H, P, S: literature, current events, history, personal, sports).

This mnemonic device will help you on test day, when you're nervous, tired, and distracted by that heavy breather sitting next to you.

Jot down the letters at the bottom of your test booklet and list examples you can use in each category. Your outline, in the wee margins of your essay booklet, should look like the following:

Always circle and define the key words in the essay assignment before you begin writing.

```
L

C

H

P

S
```

STEP 4: CHOOSE YOUR EXAMPLES

After you've jotted down the potentials, choose your strongest examples to write about. If you have two strong examples, use the traditional essay structure. If you have one strong and one slightly weaker example, use the sandwich structure. If you only have a personal example, write in the narrative structure. And, if you can't come up with anything, make a story up about your mother and use the narrative form! Remember, you're a number on a piece of paper to these graders—there's no reason you can't exaggerate or embellish (or even completely fabricate!) the details of your life.

Putting this into practice, note my outline in response to the assignment: *"Is compromise always the best way to resolve a conflict?"*

Write **L**-ittle **C**-hildren **H**-ave **P**-lay **S**-ets on your scrap paper or in the margin and fill in your potential supporting examples. Choose your best examples to include in your essay.

*HELIOCENTRIC
Having or relating to the sun as center

OUTLINE (L-ITTLE C-HILDREN H-AVE P-LAY S-ETS):

- **L**–*The Scarlet Letter*: Hester Prynne's refusal to compromise and reveal the name of Pearl's father.
- **C**–Aung San Suu Kyi's refusal to compromise her position regarding the Burmese dictatorship.
- **H**–Galileo's refusal to compromise with the Catholic Church and renounce his heliocentric* findings.
- **P**–Can't think of
- **S**–Can't think of

TOPIC SELECTION: Literature and History
STRUCTURE: Traditional

Notice that I did not have examples from every category. You, too, may not have examples for each category. I did, though, have a strong example from history and a strong example from literature. Therefore, I chose to use the traditional essay structure. Your selection of examples will help you determine which essay structure to use, so outlining before you write is essential!

This outline is meant to take one or two minutes only. But it is worth the time! I don't want you crossing your last T and dotting your last I only to have a feeling of dread set in when you realize you should have written about so and so. Equally awful is the nausea-producing experience of reaching the end of your second paragraph and realizing you have nothing left to write about.

Aside from the hive-inducing anxiety that it causes, writing before reasoning results in disorganized and faulty logic. Faulty logic is not so convincing and therefore not so high-scoring. It does not matter how great your pre-selected details may be. If you do not plan your attack, these details are not presented in a convincing manner and become useless. You must take the time to organize your thoughts before you jump into an essay, especially a persuasive essay!

Your selection of examples will help determine which essay structure to use.

"Success is not measured by what you accomplish, but by the opposition you have encountered."

ORISON SWETT MARDEN, 19TH CENTURY AMERICAN WRITER

CHAPTER 8

ADDRESS YOUR ENEMIES

Ah! The home stretch. You're almost done with your essay. Just scribble down two more sentences and you can stretch those tired little fingers of yours.

Not so fast . . . .

The final sentences that conclude your essay will be the last thing a grader will read before scoring your essay. So, you don't want the same old restate-the-thesis-and-summarize-the-main-points paragraph that most writers will throw together. You want to write an impressive and persuasive conclusion that will leave an impact on the grader.

The secret to writing a killer conclusion: address your enemies.

Those picky critics—the graders—are looking for loopholes in your logic, faulty reasoning, error in your argument. Your entire essay, at its very core, is a persuasive essay. Your job is to do just that—persuade.

You've chosen your stance. You've provided detailed examples and substantial support. Now, you've got to truly win over the graders. You've got to anticipate their objections to your arguments and systematically shoot these objections down.

Systematically shoot down the opposing arguments of your "enemies."

BRING UP AND KNOCK DOWN YOUR OPPOSITION.

> *Mention and refute your opposition in the conclusion.*

In the final paragraph of your essay, you must mention and refute the opposing side of your argument.

For example:

ASSIGNMENT: *"Should we pay more attention to people who are older and more experienced than we are?"*

THESIS: With time comes experience, and with experience comes problem-solving abilities. People should value this experience and learn from the mistakes and successes of those who came before us.

OPPOSITION: New technology and new ideas are the creative sparks that ignite progress in our society, so we can't and shouldn't rely on our elders.

REBUTTAL: However, the creation of new technology and the development of new ideas are based on old methodologies and past philosophies.

ASSIGNMENT: *"Can we learn anything valuable from fiction or is reality more important?"*

THESIS: Through literature, we are provided with universal themes that allow us to explore ourselves and the world in which we live.

OPPOSITION: Reality and hands-on experience are the only ways to truly understand a situation. Burying ourselves in fictional characters and fantasy lands only masks our problems.

REBUTTAL: However, reality offers limited and biased views. Fiction allows us to see how others might solve a problem, to grapple with reality, and to fully assess our situation.

Notice that both rebuttal sentences include the word "however." This transitional word sets up the contrast that is about to follow and prepares the reader for your rebuttal. Be sure to include "however" or a similar transitional word/phrase from the following list:

GOOD CONTRAST TRANSITIONS

Others would say . . . but . . .

Some, though, disagree . . . . However . . .

Although some might believe . . . in actuality . . .

Nevertheless, others feel . . . but . . .

A FULL CONCLUSION MUST:

• address and rebut the arguments of the opposite side

• summarize your points

• take the topic into the "now"

• sum up your essay in a sentence or two that rewords the essay prompt

---

Note the following exemplary conclusion, written by a former student, in response to: *"Should those who say what they think when no one else has the courage to say it be considered heroes?"*

> *Heroes don't only exist in the imaginary world of comic books. Heroes are also ordinary people who, in times of distress, risk ridicule, isolation and even death in order to fight for their cause. Some people would consider only those who are extraordinarily strong or brave, like the soldiers in Iraq, to be heroic. However, sometimes speaking up is the bravest act of all.*

Now, if you want to really leave a lasting impression and take your conclusion to the next level, broaden your essay and bring it to the "now." Include a sentence about a personal experience or current event that illustrates your thesis and brings your essay into present day. By doing so, the reader is forced to relate your essay to today. Notice in the prior conclusion, the war in Iraq is brought in to impact the reader.

And here's another example:

VACILLATE
Waver

> *Both Atticus Finch and Galileo demonstrate the defining characteristic of a hero: they refused to bow to pressure or refrain from speaking out against injustice. This courageous feat is the mark of a true hero. A hero cannot vacillate* in his opinions. He must be firm and resolute. We see this sort of heroism in today's society through Aung San Suu Kyi's actions. This Burmese woman has been under strict house arrest after speaking out against the injustices of her dictatorial government. She has endured her punishment but has refused to back down. She continues to speak out today, heroically. Through literature, history and a hero of today we see that speaking out shows true courage.*

Notice how the essay broadens out at the end and includes Aung Suu San Kyi, a modern and real-life hero. She is not just dropped into the essay, though. The writer transitions, prepares the reader, and then brings in Kyi. You, too, must transition gracefully when introducing a current event. The following transitions will allow you to "modernize" your conclusion and bring in a current event:

GOOD CONCLUSION TRANSITIONS

Even today, this same situation is seen . . .

Events today embody this same philosophy.

My own personal experience also illustrates that . . .

People today also show us that . . .

Today's society practices this same . . .

Bear in mind, though, that your fancy-schmancy conclusion should still include a summary of your main points and a restatement of your thesis. Also bear in mind that it will be a full paragraph. Be sure to allocate enough space: you're given two sheets of paper, only. So keep the loopy handwriting in check and save some space! I recommend practicing writing your essay on actual essay paper online at CollegeBoard.com and in College Board's book, *The Official SAT Study Guide*.

Now, of course, I know you have good intentions. I know you will map out your essay, delve into your pre-selected topics, and include pre-selected details. But, I also know that there are only twenty-five minutes. And, even if you outline and plan your essay, there is always the lingering threat of running out of time. Don't panic!

If you encounter this worst-case scenario, you must wrap up your essay and you must wrap it up fast. An essay without any sort of conclusion is considered an unfinished essay and will lose points. Therefore, simply sum up your essay in a sentence or two by rewording the essay prompt. It's not fancy, and it won't earn you extra points, but it won't cost you points either.

Last, if you choose to write in the narrative structure, remember that the conclusion should include your clearly stated thesis. The conclusion is the most important paragraph of the narrative essay because it does provide this thesis and explains how your anecdote epitomizes the essay prompt. Be sure to broaden and abstract your anecdote in the conclusion so your story applies to more than just you.

Map out your essay and leave yourself time to write a formal conclusion.

Always "wrap up" and finish your essay, even if it's just one sentence.

To sum up, after you've structured a sound essay and included the juicy details, don't forget the "knock 'em dead," comprehensive, cohesive, and convincing conclusion. So as you approach the last few lines of essay paper, take a deep breath: it ain't over yet. You still have to write a thoughtful and engaging conclusion.

Do not get sloppy at the end of your essay. Take the time to include details and style. You're only moving on to hours of multiple-choice questions, so there is no need to rush!

"The world is governed more by appearance than realities so that it is fully as necessary to seem to know something as to know it."
DANIEL WEBSTER, AMERICAN STATESMAN

CHAPTER 9

SEAL THE DEAL

After revealing most of my secrets, I am now confident that you can write a logically organized, fully supported, well-developed, stylistically enticing, powerfully persuasive essay that engages and impacts the reader. However, it never hurts to "seal the deal." The following are four easy ways to do just that.

Throw in the word *integrity**. Integrity can be the ultimate vocabulary key and can save you lots of time on the SAT essay. Look at the fifteen core topics—the word *integrity* relates to nearly all of them! You can easily construct a well-developed and detailed paragraph that revolves around the integrity of a hero, the integrity of a wise person, of a sacrifice, and so on.

*INTEGRITY
Soundness of moral character; honesty

Therefore, when brainstorming for examples and filling out your essay outline, keep *integrity* in mind! You can weasel this little word into most essays, regardless of essay structure. The word integrity will help you organize your response and craft your paragraphs. Without wasting much time, you'll be able to fill up a big chunk of space on your essay paper.

For example, note the following topic sentences that lead a reader into a paragraph about intregrity.

- *Oskar Schindler acted with integrity when he hid the Jews from the Nazis.*
- *Atticus Finch was guided by integrity when he accepted Tom Robinson's case and went against community norms.*

- *Galileo refused to sacrifice his integrity when he denied the Catholic Church's request to repeal his astronomical findings.*
- *As a global community, we must act with integrity and put aside our own selfish concerns to address the problem of world climate change.*

SECRET #9

REMEMBER THE WORD INTEGRITY—THIS WORD FITS INTO MANY ESSAY QUESTIONS.

Always pick the moral side of the argument.

Throwing in the word *integrity* and relating integrity to your thesis also establishes a "moral high ground" within your essay. By relating your thesis to integrity, you're asserting that your position is one of honor, respect, ethics, and good conscience. I'll admit, it's a dirty trick: how can readers take the dishonorable, disrespectful, unethical, soulless side of the argument? They can't . . . .

So, again: No matter which structure you choose, the SAT is at heart a persuasive essay. The word *integrity* is, in itself, persuasive. Develop your essay around integrity and establish a moral high ground in your essay to really win the reader over.

Deliberately insert some great vocabulary. Although *integrity* is truly the top-secret vocabulary word for the SAT essay, it doesn't hurt to include a few extra vocabulary words as icing on the cake because, let's face it, big words are impressive.

*AUDACITY
Boldness

*INTRACTABILITY
Not easily manipulated

*OSTENTATIOUS
Showy

*UBIQUITOUSLY
Universally

*DOCILE
Tame

*ACQUIESCE
Comply

*DISCERNINGLY
Insightfully

Her audacity* and intractability* were ostentatious*; it was known ubiquitously* that she was docile* and would soon acquiesce.*

See what I mean? Vocabulary grabs your attention and makes you think, "Wow!" Wow-factor aside, that sentence is absolutely awful. Never try to force too many vocabulary words into one sentence! Rather, sprinkle. Discerningly* include vocabulary throughout your essay.

At sixteen, your over-three-syllable-with-Latin-roots vocabulary collection may be a bit slim. For the record, the prior nastiness translates into: *Her crazy behavior was a vain display; everyone knows she's a nice little girl.* For those of you who had no clue as to the translation, don't worry about it! The secret is to write your essay without stressing over vocabulary and to leave yourself two minutes to spare.

In those two precious moments, proofread your essay. As you're proofreading, try to exchange some of your little words for big words. Substituting in three to five vocabulary words is like pulling a rabbit out of a hat. Your essay will be taking bows for you! This trick requires that you actually know some vocabulary, though. So pre-select some vocabulary words and try to fit these words into every essay. And don't pick words like *ornithologist* to know. Yeah, it looks fancy, but how often will you bring up a person who studies birds in your essay?

One method of ensuring that you include some souped-up vocab in your essay is to select a vocabulary word for each of your pre-selected examples from history and literature. If you're planning on writing about George Washington, plan to include the word *sagacious** in the essay. If you choose to know all about the Scientific Revolution, try to fit the word *heretical** in the essay. Include your pre-selected words on your historical moments and literary charts so that you can study these words! See Chapter 6 for more information about the charts.

The following is a list of vocabulary words that you can easily substitute into your essay.

- *Abhor* instead of **dislike intensely**
- *Ameliorate* instead of **make better**
- *Copious* instead of **a lot of**
- *Elated* instead of **happy**
- *Enigmatic* instead of **mysterious**
- *Exacerbate* instead of **worsen**
- *Genial* instead of **kind**
- *Heinous* instead of **terrible**

Spend two minutes proofing your essay.

Write your essay and then substitute in three to five SAT-quality vocabulary words.

*SAGACIOUS
Wise

*HERETICALLY
Sacrilegious, against the Church

- *Insipid* instead of **boring**
- *Intrepid* instead of **brave**
- *Laudatory* instead of **respectable**
- *Paltry* instead of **insignificant/scant**
- *Paradigm* instead of **model**
- *Paradoxically* instead of **on the contrary/on the other hand**
- *Pedestrian* instead of **ordinary**
- *Perspicacious/acute* instead of **smart**
- *Proliferate* instead of **grow/increase**
- *Pulchritude* instead of **beauty**
- *Spurious* instead of **wrong/false**
- *Ubiquitous/omnipresent* instead of **everywhere/universal**
- *Urbane* instead of **sophisticated**
- *Wary* instead of **cautious**

Please realize that vocabulary is only an added bonus. Your priority is to finish your essay, not to try to include the longest, most-difficult-to-pronounce word possible. Strong examples, a powerful thesis, and directional topic sentences—all written stylistically—are what will earn you a top score. Adding impressive vocabulary words is only an option if you've accomplished all of that with time to spare.

Also, be aware that vocabulary is only impressive if it is used correctly in a sentence. Be sure you understand the various forms of your vocabulary word (noun form, adjective form, verb form) and that you completely understand the definition of your word. Memorize the spelling, as well!

Write legibly and neatly. Throwing in the word *integrity* and some other eye-catching "big words" will help you look the part of a sophisticated writer. But you also have to make sure your handwriting looks the part of a sophisticated writer, too.

There's no Times New Roman or Comic Sans to save those of you with poor handwriting. It is absolutely crucial that your essay be neat and legible. If graders can't read your essay, they can't give it a high score. So slow down and make sure you dot your I's and cross your T's. And on a side note: the extra "girly"

Bring an extra eraser to the test.

writing, so to speak, with the heart over the "I" and the super-loopy tail on the "Y" and "G," should be avoided. You want to be seen as a mature writer. Hearts all over your paper won't help your cause.

That being said, neatness does count. If you're writing legibly but every other word is scribbled out—with notes in the margins, asterisks, and inserts—your essay looks like a warzone. If you had to draw arrows for the reader to follow to the next paragraph or things are written sideways down the left margin, your essay becomes a headache. To prevent this, take the two minutes at the start of the essay to organize your writing and outline! As I have mentioned (Secret #7), before you begin writing, you need to make an outline! Organize your thoughts; choose your examples; decide which structure you'll be writing in! Remember: **L**-ittle **C**-hildren **H**-ave **P**-lay **S**-ets.

I do realize that regardless of the outline, mapping, and preparation you've done for the essay, while you're racing the clock, you may happen to make a mistake. When this happens, put a single line through the "mess-up." Don't scratch it out Tasmanian-devil style so that there's a giant black blob in the middle of a sentence. These blobs are distracting, and readers will lose focus. A single line will do the trick! Of course, you'll be writing in pencil, so you can always erase (if you've got the time). Be sure to bring a good eraser to the test, one of those big, not-attached-to-the-pencil erasers.

Write in clear, standard English. Just as you should avoid juvenile handwriting, scribbles, and doodles, you should avoid juvenile language. Try to avoid using contractions. Rather than *isn't* use *is not*, and rather than *should've* use *should have*, etc. Also, avoid any slang or informal writing. You ain't gonna score high if ya essay is full o' slang and informalities!

Last, this is your essay. Unless you're writing about a personal experience, take out the *I* and *you* and address your audience in third person.

Avoid juvenile handwriting and juvenile language.

Once again, an excellent essay needs to look the part. A clean, neat paper, written in proper English *looks* like a good essay and leaves the grader with a good first impression. And, by using the secrets in this book, your essay will certainly sound like a good essay (a great essay, even!). If it looks like a good essay and sounds like a good essay—it is a good essay, and it will receive a top score.

CHAPTER 10

MAKE IT BRAINLESS

Unless you're a child genius with a photographic memory, you might still be feeling a bit overwhelmed. Although I'd love for you to know every single teensy-weensy element that goes into a perfect twenty-five-minute essay, I also recognize that you might be freaking out!

Be sure to go back and re-read specific chapters or sections that you know you need to work on. If transitions aren't your thing—well, darling, make them your thing: practice, practice, practice. You should write several essays before you show up on test day. So put the pencil to the paper, because although practice may not actually make perfect, it will get you fairly close.

I do realize, though, that practicing at home involves lounging around in a comfortable environment without a proctor pacing to and fro, without the pressure of an actual grade, and without the haziness of an early Saturday morning. So what happens if you're nervous, stressed, and overtired? What happens if you freeze on test day?

The opening paragraph of an essay can be the hardest to write. It's the first impression. It sets the reader's expectations. You want to write it right! The secret to avoiding a test-day catastrophe: rely on a template to make the writing process simple, automated, and completely brainless. In fact, for those of you anxious, nail-biting test takers, rely on a template for the entire essay.

RELY ON THE BRAINLESS ESSAY TEMPLATE TO GET YOU THROUGH A TEST-DAY BRAIN FREEZE.

The Stress-free Start

The "brainless introduction" ensures that you avoid writer's block while simultaneously scoring some points. Once you have the introduction down, you can move on to your pre-selected examples and details.

> **THE BRAINLESS INTRODUCTION TEMPLATE**
>
> • one-word sentence
> • definition
> • introduction of body paragraph topics
> • thesis

Memorize the brainless essay introduction to avoid a "freak-out" on test day.

On test day, if you can't figure out where to begin, stop figuring. In fact, stop thinking altogether and rely on the following steps to brainlessly construct an opening paragraph. Follow these steps.

STEP 1:

Circle the key word—the word that best relates to the core topic—within the assignment. See Chapter 2.

STEP 2:

Write that circled key word down, followed by a period. Bam—a one-word hook that is sure to grab the reader's attention. See Chapter 5.

For example, if you had a hero question, your first sentence would be "Hero." If you had a sacrifice question, your first sentence would be "Sacrifice."

STEP 3:

Define your one-word sentence. Quantify the vague term or concept mentioned in the essay assignment. See Chapter 5.

STEP 4:

Introduce the examples you will use to support your position. See Chapter 6.

STEP 5:

State your position. Are you agreeing or disagreeing with the quote? Your position should be stated as a stand-alone thesis sentence. See Chapter 3.

To make it *completely* brainless, memorize the sentence below.

> *(X) and (Y) offer (copious/myriad/a plethora of) examples showing (thesis).*

This sentence not only introduces your topics, it also incorporates vocabulary! Choose whichever vocabulary word you like best: *copious*, *myriad*, or *plethora*. All three words mean *many*.

X and Y are the areas from which you will be drawing support. If you are including *To Kill a Mockingbird* and Martin Luther in your essay, then X would be literature and Y would be history. Your clearly stated thesis should be stated after you've introduced your supporting examples.

For example:

Brainless, but impressive, introduction:

> *Originality. Originality is the unique perspective and novel thoughts that creators, designers, thinkers, artists, and everyone else contribute. History and literature offer copious examples of uniqueness and originality, showing that people's differing opinions bring about originality and creativity.*

The Brainless Breeze-through Body

The brainless introduction should be followed by a body paragraph about (in this case) the Renaissance and a second body paragraph about *To Kill a Mockingbird*. Start with a topic sentence (main idea + direction) and then follow through with specifics. End your body paragraph by restating the thesis. This will keep the readers focused on your argument.

Transition and repeat. Remember, a traditional essay requires two fully developed body paragraphs.

The Fuss-free Finish

It's sometimes just as hard to finish an essay as it is to begin. But ending a brainless essay is, well, brainless. So memorize the following formula.

> **THE BRAINLESS CONCLUSION TEMPLATE**
>
> · restate the thesis
> · present the opposition: discuss the other side of the argument (in one or two sentences)
> · rebut the opposition: explain why the opposing side is incorrect.
> · broaden and bring it to the now: relate your argument to the present day.

Review Chapter 8 to fully understand how to create a strong, persuasive conclusion in just minutes.

I've included the brainless essay template on the next page. Memorize this template so that if you're unsure or are having a slight nervous breakdown the day of the test, you'll still be able to write a powerful introduction, fluidly move into your body paragraphs, and write a powerful conclusion.

With a little memorization, you'll create a thoughtful, logical, organized, cohesive, detailed, stylistic, engaging, vocabulary-filled, high-scoring essay—brainlessly!

BRAINLESS ESSAY

BRAINLESS INTRODUCTION

One-word Sentence
Pull out the key term in the essay question.

Definition of Key Term
Define your one-word sentence.

Introduction of Topics
Address the complexities of the essay question, introduce your supporting examples, and throw in a little vocab! (*Myriad, copious,* or *plethora* can be fit into an introductory sentence.)

Thesis
Couple your main idea and key points with direction.

> Formula: One-word hook. Definition. (X) and (Y) offer (copious/myriad/a plethora of) examples showing (thesis).

BODY PARAGRAPH #1: LITERATURE
Must have at least two or three supporting details—avoid plot summary! Bring in a quote.

> Topic Sentence: *Main Idea + Direction*

BODY PARAGRAPH #2: HISTORY
A transition is essential! Must have at least two or three supporting details—avoid superficial overview! Bring in a date or time frame.

> Topic Sentence: *Transition + Main Idea + Direction*

BRAINLESS CONCLUSION

Restate the Thesis
Present your argument in one sentence.

Present the Opposition
Discuss the other side of the argument (in one or two sentences).

Rebut the Opposition
Explain why the opposing side is incorrect.

Broaden and Bring to the Now
Relate your argument to the present day.

"Play by the rules, but be ferocious."
PHIL KNIGHT, CO-FOUNDER OF NIKE

CHAPTER 11

PUT IT ALL TOGETHER: WIN THE SAT ESSAY GAME

I've revealed all of my secrets. You now know the insider "magic" and can now easily write a top-scoring SAT essay. Each secret helps prepare you by bringing you closer to a pre-written essay for test day. Now you have to do your part. As your coach, I have given you direction, given you guidelines, and given you strategy. But now you need to be a good player. These little secrets won't get you very far unless you put them all together. I want mixing, melding, blending, concocting, using, and abusing! A stellar conclusion without a detailed body will not get you that above-average score. A few vocabulary words sprinkled into a paragraph that lacks any of the elements of style—not gonna cut it!

You must put in some preparation time before test day. You must put all the secrets together on test day to guarantee a top essay score.

Ten Secrets to Add 100 Points to Your SAT Essay Score

1. You can answer the question before test day.
2. You can predict the SAT essay question.
3. Construct a rock-solid, stand-alone sentence that answers the essay question and summarizes your essay's main point.
4. Know the type of house you will be constructing before you begin to build.

5. Entice the reader with style and wow the reader with the first sentence.

6. Pre-select your supporting examples and memorize five facts about each.

7. Do not start writing until you've outlined your supporting body examples.

8. Bring up and knock down your opposition.

9. Remember the word *integrity*—this word fits into many essay questions.

10. Rely on the brainless essay template to get you through a test-day brain freeze.

Secrets are fun, so let's make this a game. (Yes, it's the SAT, so it might not be as fun as the Wii or Yahtzee, but try to imagine.) Like any game, the SAT essay has an objective: achieving a top score. It also has rules: two pages only; handwritten; pencil. And it has a time limit: twenty-five minutes. Last, like any good game, the SAT essay can be beaten. So, put on your game face. Play to win.

The clock starts; game on. Please note that most games do in fact have a built-in timer, buzzer, or sand-filled hourglass. The SAT, though, is a bit more unpredictable. You are given twenty-five minutes, but you may not have a clock in the test room to look at. Therefore, you must wear a watch on test day so that you can allocate your twenty-five minutes appropriately. Again, you must wear a watch on test day!

Wear a watch on test day.

SO, TWENTY-FIVE MINUTES . . .

1. Read the essay prompt. Underline and define the key words.

2. Outline using the mnemonic device "**L**-ittle **C**-hildren **H**-ave **P**-lay **S**-ets."

3. Decide which format fits your outline, topic, and your details.

TWENTY-THREE MINUTES . . .

4. Begin with a bang! Choose the brainless introduction or choose another of the suggested, attention-grabbing hooks.

5. Define the key words from the assignment (the key words that relate to the core topics).

6. Develop a stand-alone thesis that definitively answers the essay assignment, introduces your supporting examples, and charts the direction of your essay.

EIGHTEEN MINUTES . . .

7. Beginning with a strong topic sentence, detail and develop your first supporting example.

ELEVEN MINUTES . . .

8. Choose a strong transition to move you to your next example.

9. Again, compose a strong topic sentence that details and develops your second supporting example.

SEVEN MINUTES . . .

10. Summarize your argument. Bring up and knock down your opposition.

11. Include a current event (if possible) to really end powerfully.

12. End the essay.

TWO MINUTES . . .

13. Proofread your essay.

14. Swap out five words for SAT vocabulary.

Put your pencil down. Take a deep breath. Wipe your brow. Throw yourself a silent little party and pat yourself on the back. You just wrote a top-scoring essay in only twenty-five minutes.

To make sure you're ready to play to win, look over and review my top secrets and key essay strategies. Rather than hunting through the book, I've pulled them out and created a handy-dandy review sheet. This handy-dandy is found on the next page. Photocopy it! Keep a copy in your pocket, a copy under your pillow, a copy in your locker, and a copy on your refrigerator door. Heck, send one to your dentist so that, should you have a toothache a week before the test, you can still be studying!

THE SAT ESSAY KEY STRATEGIES

Use this sheet as a handy, quick reminder of how to write it right!

BEFORE THE TEST
Fully prepare ahead of time.
- Memorize the fifteen core topics.
- Know the details for two literary works, three current events, three historical moments, three personal experiences, and/or three sports moments. Do *not* use the Holocaust, MLK, Jr., or September 11 as a primary supporting detail.
- Memorize **L**-ittle **C**-hildren **H**-ave **P**-lay **S**-ets as a trick to remember the detail categories above. If you can't think of anything to write, write a story about your mother (feel free to make it up)!
- Feel comfortable using each essay structure:
   o Traditional: intro (thesis here), detail A, detail B, conclusion
   o Sandwich: detail A (thesis here), detail B, detail A
   o Narrative: begin "in the moment" and clearly state your thesis in the conclusion (strict formula!)

ON TEST DAY
Read the question carefully and focus your essay on answering this question.
- Respond to the assignment, not the excerpt.
- Underline the key words.
- Define the key words in your introduction.
- Always take a clear position (agree or disagree—nothing in the middle).
- Begin with a *bang*!

Detail and develop your argument
- Spend two or three minutes outlining your essay: **L**-ittle **C**-hildren **H**-ave **P**-lay **S**-ets.
- Follow the formulas for thesis and topic sentences.
- Do *not* write a plot summary of a literary work!
- Remember the word *integrity*—it fits into many essay questions.
- *Always* use interesting transitions between paragraphs.
- Show, don't tell: include the five elements of style this book recommends.

End Powerfully
- Bring up and shoot down your opposition.
- Include a current event or personal experience (if possible) to impact the reader.
- Wrap up! It is perfectly fine to end the essay by restating the quote or question if you're out of time.

Pay attention to time
- Memorize the brainless essay template to avoid a "freak out."
- Fill your *two* pages: more writing = higher score.
- Spend two minutes proofreading your essay at the end.

Write for your audience
- Substitute in some SAT vocabulary words.
- Write legibly and neatly.
- Don't use jargon or slang.

"Practice does not make perfect. Perfect practice makes perfect."
UNKNOWN

CHAPTER 12

IT'S YOUR TURN

Now that you've put in some work, broken a sweat, used some elbow grease, and *truly* prepared for this essay (memorized the fifteen core topics, assembled your examples and details, and are comfortable with the three essay formats) you can compose and evaluate your writing.

Use the following recent SAT essay assignments to construct your own twenty-five-minute SAT essay! Keep your reference sheets handy for the first few essays you write to remind yourself of what goes into a great essay. Be sure to time yourself. You'll only get twenty-five minutes for the "real deal," so only give yourself twenty-five minutes for the practice essays. Also, remember that your essay should fill two pages. Fill two pages, but do not write more than two pages!

I strongly recommend that you compose at least one essay for each core topic listed. This is only 375 minutes of your entire life span. Not much time at all! Don't be discouraged if you run out of time the first time you try this. Perfect practice makes for perfection. Try again. Each time will be easier.

I've also included some essay-scoring guidelines. After you've written an essay, use these guidelines to self-assess your writing. Also use the guidelines when you score the real sample SAT essays in the next chapter, which are marked to show you the most important features for which a grader looks. So, get ready (paper, notes, pencil, watch), get set (take a deep breath), choose your topic, and *write*!

Core Topic Essay Questions

CHOICES/MAKING DECISIONS

- *"Should people make more of an effort to keep some things private?"*
- *"Are bad choices and good choices equally likely to have negative consequences?"*

COMPETITION/COOPERATION

- *"Can a group of people function effectively without someone being in charge?"*
- *"Do people achieve more success by cooperation than by competition?"*

Fill two pages, but do not write more than two pages!

CONFLICT

- *"Can any obstacle or disadvantage be turned into something good?"*
- *"Do you think that ease does not challenge us and that we need adversity to show us who we really are?"*

CONSCIENCE/ETHICS

- *"Outrageous behavior is instructive. It reveals to us the limits of our tolerance."*
- *"Is conscience a more powerful motivator than money, fame, or power?"*

CREATIVITY

- *"Is creativity needed more than ever in the world today?"*
- *"Does planning interfere with creativity?"*

GROUP/INDIVIDUAL

- *"Is the opinion of the majority—in government or in any other circumstances—a poor guide?"*
- *"Is it always best to determine one's own views of right and wrong, or can we benefit from following a crowd?"*

HAPPINESS

- *"Is it better to change one's attitude than to change one's circumstances?"*
- *"Is it more important to do work that one finds fulfilling or work that pays well?"*

HEROISM

- *"Should we admire heroes but not celebrities?"*
- *"Do people learn who they are only when they are forced into action?"*

MOTIVATION

- *"What motivates people to change?"*
- *"Is it important to try to understand people's motivations before judging their actions?"*

PERFECTION

- *"Do you think that perfection is not interesting and that it is the flaws that count?"*
- *"Can people achieve success only if they aim to be perfect?"*

PERSPECTIVE/TRUTH

- *"Would the world be a better place if everyone always told the complete truth?"*
- *"Is the way something seems to be not always the same as it actually is?"*

SACRIFICE

- *"Do all established traditions deserve to remain in existence?"*
- *"Is it best not to sacrifice our ideas, opinions, or behaviors?"*

SUCCESS

- *"Is persistence more important than ability in determining a person's success?"*
- *"Are people more likely to be productive and successful when they ignore the opinions of others?"*

TECHNOLOGY

- *"Has today's abundance of information only made it more difficult for us to understand the world around us?"*
- *"Is the world changing for the better?"*

WISDOM

- *"Can knowledge be a burden rather than a benefit?"*
- *"Should we pay more attention to people who are older and more experienced than we are?"*

ESSAY SCORING GUIDE

Two individuals grade each essay, which receives a score of 0-6 from each grader. These two scores are then summed to calculate the final essay score, out of 12.

Score of 6

This is the "masterful" essay. It's a pretty darn good essay for twenty-five minutes of writing, but it's not an essay worthy of publication or a prize. Anyone can score a 6 on the SAT essay! A score of 6 is granted if your essay:

• Is organized and easy to follow.
• Exhibits sentence variety and a strong vocabulary.
• Is for the most part free of any spelling or grammatical errors.
• Clearly answers the essay question, using specific and detailed examples and reasons.
• Explores fully the complexities of the essay question, showing outstanding critical thinking.

Score of 5

This is a great essay with a few too many grammatical or spelling errors or an awkward/ undeveloped paragraph somewhere. A score of 5 means that your essay:

• Is organized and easy to follow.
• Exhibits sentence variety and a decent vocabulary.
• Has some obvious spelling or grammatical errors.
• Clearly answers the essay question, using general examples and reasoning.
• Provides appropriate, but not outstanding, support.

Score of 4

This is an essay that looks, for the most part, like every other essay the reader has read. Oftentimes, this essay lacks stylistic elements or lacks a fully cohesive, logical argument. Transitional or topic sentences may be missing. It fulfills the requirements, but it's a standard, boring essay. Specific examples may be presented, but these examples are not fully developed. This essay is adequate.

Score of 3

This is a so-so essay. It looks like most of the other essays: the intro is a boring paraphrase of the essay prompt, the examples are overused and nonspecific. Organization isn't terrific (thesis, topic, or sentences are missing) so the essay is somewhat coherent but lacks flow. Plot summary, rather than sophisticated analysis, is often included within the body paragraphs.

Scores of 2, 1, or 0

Either you didn't write an essay, wrote an essay on how to make chocolate-chip cookies in German, or tried to answer the essay question in three sentences.

"Good critical writing is measured by the perception and evaluation of its subject."
RAYMOND CHANDLER, AMERICAN NOVELIST AND SCREENWRITER

CHAPTER 13

EVALUATE PEER ESSAYS FOR PRACTICE

Now it's time for you to practice grading actual SAT essays written by students like you. Well, not *just* like you because some of them weren't in the know about how to write essays that stood out from the rest. Some of the essays are average, others are pretty good, and others are superb.

The essays are already annotated. They point out the major features that the graders will be searching for. You'll be able to see what makes a fabulous essay fabulous. (And what makes a not-so-fabulous essay, well, not so fabulous.)

Remember, you are aiming for a score of 9 or higher.

Use this chapter as a learning tool. Study the effective techniques used by other students so that you can incorporate them into a strong essay of your own. Note that some of the included essays will score below 9. Obviously don't incorporate those techniques, but you can learn from others' mistakes.

On test day, two readers will evaluate your essay. Each spends just a few minutes reading through your essay and gives it a score from 1-6. The two scores are then combined to create an overall essay score. In other words, a perfect SAT essay rates a 12. Once again, you want a score of 9 or higher.

Just for fun, try to grade them. Use the scoring rubric provided to assess these essays, as well as your own practice essays. (Actual test-day scores for each example essay start on page 150.)

P. S. These essays are "as is," and may contain grammatical or spelling errors. Can you find them?

SAMPLE ESSAYS

ESSAY 1: Traditional Essay

PROMPT: *"Are those who pursue individual goals more successful than those who pursue a common goal?"*

CORE TOPIC: Cooperation

A one-word sentence is an excellent opener!

(Success.) Success has different meanings to different people. The most success is brought about when an individual works hard at pursing his or her own personal goals. Literature and current events offer a (myriad) of examples.

Good vocab!

In To Kill A Mockingbird by Harper Lee the community was divided into two clearly defined groups—black and white. However, Atticus Finch refused to associate with one of these groups, and stood alone. Atticus was the moral voice of this novel because he held no biases and was able to mediate between the different groups. He represented Tom Robinson during the rape trial. Although the white community despised Atticus for representing a black man accused of rape, Atticus refused to lose his (integrity.) Although Tom Robinson was wrongly convicted and executed, Atticus was successful at educating a town and lessening the division that separated the community. Because Atticus followed his individual goals and never lost his integrity, Atticus was successful.

Weak topic sentence that sets up plot summary.

Excellent word to develop in an essay.

The success brought about by pursuing individual goals is also seen today. This week in Time Magazine I read about a real life hero named Chawang Norphel. He was a civil engineer—part of a bigger picture—but he was encouraged to follow his own goals and has successfully saved a community in Asia. Global warming has caused a melting of the glaciers between the tract of land between Pakistan and Asia. Chawang invented an artificial glacier that the community could affordably use. Chawang Norphel, the iceman, was able to save a community by pursing his own personal interests.

Bringing in a current event broadens the essay and brings it to the "now."

Atticus and Norphel showed leadership by breaking away from the larger group and following their personal interests. Success is attained not by a group working towards a common goal, because people in groups tend to pass up opportunities and rely on other people. Rather, true success is accomplished by individuals who follow their passions.

Addresses and rebuts the opposition.

ESSAY 2: Traditional Essay

PROMPT: *"Are those who pursue individual goals more successful than those who pursue a common goal?"*

CORE TOPIC: Cooperation

Starting with detail grabs the reader's attention.

Jean Jacques Rousseau preached a "general will" in most of his writings. The general will was an idea that was larger than any individual, man or woman. It was an idea that was meant to be for the good of the nation, group or organization as a whole. Karl Marx subsequently worked off Rousseau's ideas to formulate communism, in which everything is owned by the state and in essence the government is the general will. Although communism was not successful in the USSR, it did promote the general will. Holding true to the mantra of general will, the most successful organizations in the world are those that have members who do not pursue individual goals, but rather they pursue what is good for the group as a whole. History also offers (copious) examples that show working towards a general will is most successful.

Good vocabulary.

Weak topic sentence.

Harriet Tubman was born into slavery in Maryland. She lived the horrors of what it was to be a slave. When she was just a child, her master threw a heavy block that hit her head and she had headaches and seizures for the rest of her life. She eventually managed to escape from slavery to the Free North, but because she was selfless, she organized the Underground Railroad. She returned to the south thirteen times risking being recaptured each time to save others from slavery. After the Fugitive Slave Clause was issued in (1850), she helped slaves escape even further north into Canada. The Underground Railroad would not have been successful if it were not for the intrepid and selfless nature of not just Harriet Tubman, but all who participated in the hiding and transporting of slaves to freedom. Working together brought about the Underground Railroad's success.

Including dates helps to avoid superficiality.

Great detail and development.

Good transition

Government is another example of the need for individuals to think less (provincially) and to work towards success as a functional group. Franklin Delano Roosevelt's administration and especially his implementation of

Vocab!

the New Deal is a great example of such. FDR and the members of his Cabinet were not nearly as affected by the Great Depression as other members of the country, yet he *Vocab!* (zealously) worked toward implementing public works projects and infrastructure to handle unemployment. FDR was working towards something greater than just himself—he was working for the country, and this is what led to his reelection and success as a president.

Strong conclusion that restates the main argument, summarizes the main points, and addresses the opposition. Although Harriet Tubman and Franklin Delano Roosevelt might not say they were working for the "general will," and they probably hadn't read Marx or Rousseau, the fact is that they were not working for individual goals, but rather for the greater good and that is why they were both successful.

ESSAY 3: Traditional Essay
PROMPT: *"Are those who pursue individual goals more successful than those who pursue a common goal?"*
CORE TOPIC: Cooperation

Begins with a bang and incorporates elements of style.

Success. What does it really mean to be successful? When Bette Graham invented white-out because she continuously made typing errors as a secretary, sure she was successful. When Art Fry created a bookmark that would stick to his church hymn without leaving residue, consequently creating the post-it note, sure, he too was successful. However, the most successful any group or organization can be is by individuals learning from others' previous mistakes, working assiduously to improve. WEß Dubois' success within the African American community and Galileo's success among astronomers are just two of a plethora of examples that show that success is achieved by tenacious individuals.

Great detail but awkwardly worded.

Vocab!

Vocab!

After the end of the Civil War, African Americans were granted freedom. However, they were still greatly discriminated against. Many activists emerged as leaders, trying to obtain equality. It wasn't until WEß Dubois spoke out that anything actually changed. Dubois saw that peaceful techniques were not getting anywhere. He organized the NAACP and held the Niagara Conference in attempts to persuade fellow African Americans to really speak out and do something about the unfair treatment they were experiencing. If it wasn't for his individual activism, African Americans attempts at gaining equality would have been much less successful as a whole.

Galileo is another example of a hardworking individual who learned from others' mistakes and consequently was very successful. Until Galileo, everyone believed Aristotle's geocentric theory. However, Galileo knew this theory was fundamentally flawed. He worked tenaciously and discovered that the universe was actually heliocentric. While he was debunked and called a heretic for his discovery, if it hadn't been for Galileo's determination and wisdom science would not have progressed as it has.

Vocab!

Vocab!

Vocab!

Needs a transition.

This past week I read in Time magazine about Chewang Nephel, a man who is trying to save indigent communities in Asia from global warming. While his success has not yet been determined, it was made clear in the article that he will indeed succeed at some level in the future. It is because of the hard work and determination of individuals that all groups and communities succeed.

Conclusion broadens the essay to the now but fails to restate the main points or address the opposition.

ESSAY 4: Narrative/Sandwich Essay
PROMPT: *"Are those who pursue individual goals more successful than those who pursue a common goal?"*
CORE TOPIC: Cooperation

Opening with dialogue engages the reader.

"Come on guys!" I half yelled trying to get my group to get things done. "You can't all just do what you want! We'll never finish!' We were working on a presentation, but from the looks of it we did not seem to be a group. Everyone was doing something different and not cooperating. It was our last day to work, and we accomplished nothing.

Lacking detail

I've had many experiences with groups, and that one was the worst. Everyone was pursing his/her own interests. Because of this, nothing was getting contributed to the group project and the assignment was not being completed. When members of a group don't work towards a common goal, they are the least successful.

Some believe that accepting decisions made by groups discourage the expression of individual talent. I think this statement is preposterous because groups do the exact opposite with individual talent. When in a group, one can use one's specific talent to better the group and help its cause. For example, if a group was studying Medieval Europe and one group member was an expert in this subject, he or she could be the guiding light for the team, showcasing his or her individual talent and skill in the area.

Brings up the opposition, but this should be in the conclusion.

One of my many other and much better group experiences came out of another similar project. All of the students in my group worked exceptionally well together, and we finished the project early. One student was a very good artist, and he was in charge of designing the poster. Another student had a free period during school, and she was in charge of going to the library to gather information. Each person in the group had an individual task, but these were just small parts of the whole project. It is the group that gets a project completed or a goal attained. A group is most successful **"when all of its members are not encouraged to pursue their own goals, but encouraged to work together and contribute to a common goal."**

Ends with the direct quote to really "hit home."

ESSAY 5: Traditional Essay

PROMPT: *"Are those who pursue individual goals more successful than those who pursue a common goal?"*

CORE TOPIC: Cooperation

Begins with a bang!

Success. Successes can be defined as the achievement of one's goals or overarching purpose. Oftentimes it is believed that groups or organizations are successful because their members are able to pursue their own interest. Ultimately, however, groups are most successful when they work as one; when all the members of the groups are working towards a common goal. Both literature and

Vocab!

history offer a myriad of examples that demonstrate such an argument.

Excellent definition of key terms.

In the novel, The Lord of the Flies by William Golding, a group of boys get stranded on an island and their lack of unity causes their demise. In need of organization, the boys elect a leader, Ralph, to make the rules. This decision is upsetting to some of the boys, but one in particular, Jack. Jack feels as though there is no point in maintaining civility on the island and the boys should let their inner savagery emerge. The group of boys consequently divides, each division with its own set of goals. This leads to the downfall of both groups on the island because Jack's group of "hunters" begins to accrue confidence and later arrogance. The boys who embraced savagery end up killing other boys. The pursuit of different goals is what caused the boys to live unsuccessfully on the island.

Lots of supporting detail and concrete, specific facts.

Simple but effective transition.

Similarly, the Union's success in the Civil War resulted from the army's unification. When a group is unified and its members are not pursuing their own personal wishes, more often than not the group will achieve success. The Union devised an intelligent plan in order to defeat the Confederate South. The South had a clear advantage in the army because more soldiers were trained and eager to fight. However, the North strategized and worked together, using their abundance of natural resources and powerful navy. The North was victorious after two decisive battles, the Battle of Gettysburg and the Battle of Vicksburg. General Robert E. Lee of the South surrendered to General Ulysses S.

Grant at the Appomattox Court House in 1865, ending the war. The North's success was derived from its cohesiveness.

Success results from unity. In The <u>Lord of the Flies</u>, the division that occurs in the group of boys creates discord, ultimately disabling the group from thriving. In the Civil War, the cohesiveness and ingenuity of the Union forces permitted success. Success through unity is still seen today, as groups around the world band together to fight for causes such as ending genocide in Darfur and helping with AIDS prevention in Africa. The only way to truly bring about these sweeping changes and find peace is for all of us to work together. Although some feel that unity limits diversity, it is actually unity that allows diversity to foster and communities to flourish.

Current events impact a reader.

Addresses and rebuts the opposition.

ESSAY 1: Traditional Essay
PROMPT: *"Does the truth change depending on perspective?"*
CORE TOPIC: Truth

Begins with a thought-provoking question.

How can one be certain that something is real—that something is the truth? Truth must be decided: one must take into account all available information and piece together a logical, real conclusion. Therefore, truth may change based on perspective and the evidence available. A multifaceted truth can be seen in both history and literature.

Clear thesis.

Introduces supporting examples.

Vocab!

Concrete dates are provided.

July 4th, 1776. English colonists formally declared their independence from the English monarchy overseas. Colonists argued that it was unjust to be controlled by King George thousands of miles away—a several week voyage across the Atlantic ocean. How could English parliament decide what was best for the colonists? They couldn't! Riots started when England tried to oppose increased taxes. Colonists abhorred the Tea Act and the Stamp Act, demanding that there be "no taxation without representation." To the colonists, the truth was clear: England was unjustly oppressing the rights of the American colonists. This truth presented only one option; colonists must be liberated from the tyranny of King George. The American Revolution was a war of freedom. The American Revolution was a war of rebellion, however, from the English standpoint. From this perspective, colonists were seen as ungrateful. They gladly accepted imports, the protection of the English militia, and the economy that English sea-trading offered, but they refused to contribute to the English throne; they refused to abide by English law. From this perspective, the truth was entirely different.

Excellent body details.

Vocab!

Weak topic sentence that provides no transition, direction and sets up plot summary.

George and Lennie are the main characters in Of Mice and Men by Steinbeck. Throughout the book, George protects Lennie. Lennie, unfortunately, is somewhat of a social outcast, unintentionally crossing unspoken social boundaries. He kills a puppy because he pets it too hard; he assaults a woman, Curly's wife, only because he wants to touch her soft hair. The assault escalates to murder,

Paragraph provides detail and development that focus the reader on the thesis.

(cont.) Paragraph provides detail and development that focus the reader on the thesis.

and George protects Lennie by hiding him. In the end, George is unable to conceal Lennie's whereabouts from the town that is hunting him, and George kills Lennie. From George's perspective, killing Lennie was the right thing to do. George made the ultimate sacrifice—he shot his best friend—so that Lennie would be spared the ostracizing and condemnation of society. From another perspective, George was a ruthless murderer—killing his best friend and seeking "an eye for an eye."

The truth changes depending on the point of view taken. From one perspective, the American Revolution was an inevitable fight for freedom. From another, a petty fight for power. Likewise, from one perspective, George is characterized as a martyr, killing his best friend in the world to prevent Lennie's further suffering. From another, George is cold-hearted. Truth changes depending on how a situation is approached. Indeed, "a man with one watch knows the time. A man with two watches isn't so sure."

Ends with the quote.

ESSAY 2: Traditional Essay
PROMPT: *"Does the truth change depending on perspective?"*
CORE TOPIC: Truth

Incorporates stylistic elements to lure the reader.

Truth. Is this a definite, unchanging absolute or a variable that can easily change? The answer to this question is simple. Truth can change as easily as the weather, and more often than not, does. Different people can see the same thing from a distinctly different viewpoint and, therefore, their conception of what is truth is fundamentally altered.

Begins with a bang and provides a thesis, but fails to introduce topic.

Ample detail and development.

In literature, this concept is shown in George Orwell's masterpiece, 1984. The novel describes an anti-utopia in which the truth is ever changing and history is constantly being updated. The main character, Winston Smith, works for the Ministry of Truth, a government department ironically charged with the task of modifying history to suit the needs of the government. All this effort works towards the goal of indoctrinating the minds of the people living in Oceania so that everyone's conception of the truth, and the past, is identical. However, Winston is an anomaly. He exhibits the accuracy of the aforementioned variability in truth. Winston appears to be the only sane person in his society and therefore has a distinctly different conception of truth than the impressionable masses. Even in a society that strives to exterminate all dissension and differing opinions, there is still the exception to this rule and this flaw in the government plans.

Excellent transition.

On a more current note, the Palestinian-Israeli struggle is another clear example of the ever changing truth. From its inception, Israel has almost always been at war with at least one of its Arab neighbors. In recent years, the primary threat to Israel has shifted from outside forces to Palestinian terrorist groups operating in the West Bank and Gaza Strip. Many, but obviously not all, Palestinians engage in terrorists activities. The largest terrorist group, Hamas, has gained credence and experienced a great victory in the Palestinian elections a short time ago. When a Palestinian suicide bomber strikes Israel, it is decried

Excellent detail in support of essay's argument.

(cont.) Excellent detail in support of essay's argument.

as an act of unnecessary violence by Israelis, and is considered a justifiable act in a struggle for freedom by many Palestinians. This situation calls to mind the phrase, "One man's terrorist is another man's freedom fighter." The fact that two groups of people can view the same event in such different ways is a testament to truth changing with perspective.

Another strong transition.

In summation, conception of the truth does change from person to person. These variations in "truth" may be considered undesirable, but are only reflections of the differences that exist in the global community. It is for this reason, that no matter how hard we try to make fact uniform, there will always be uncontrollable differences in one's view on what is or is not truth.

Strong restatement of main argument.

ESSAY 3: Traditional Essay
PROMPT: *"Does the truth change depending on perspective?"*
CORE TOPIC: Truth

Begins with a literal bang!

Boom! A bomb detonates in a crowded, open-air Israeli market. One group of people rejoices, while another grieves. September 11, 2001. As the World Trade Center's crumble and fall to the ground, Americans despair, while Islamic "Extremists" across the world celebrate. These scenarios are just two examples of how one man's terrorist is another man's freedom fighter. Reality is subjective; what you perceive to be true may be different than what I see as truth. Even for a meaningless football game, this comes into play. A receiver pushes a cornerback, and the cornerback pushes back harder. The receiver falls. The referee only saw the second push; Pass interference, offense. Thus, the idea of "truth" is truly dependent on the person judging it.

Details are used to effectively frame the argument.

Clear thesis statement.

Groups like Hamas, Al-Qaeda, the Tamil Tigers, and the Hezbullah have been labeled by the United States and many of her allies as "terrorists." But from many other peoples' perspectives, these "terrorists" groups are in the right, combating imperialism in their respective areas throughout the world. Well, who is telling the "truth?" Whose viewpoint is correct? In actuality, both perspectives are correct and truthful. And, looking back, even the Americans used "Terrorist" methods against the British to gain independence during the Revolutionary War. In the same way, although the United States may strongly object to the use of violence and brutality to achieve goals that may be better served by diplomacy (in areas such as Israel), the so-called "terrorists" are perfectly justified in their own minds, and the minds of their people, and therefore, their ideas are just as "true" as ours.

Thought-provoking questions engage the reader.

Good transition.

The idea of truth being relative extends to all facets of society. In a 2005 football game in which the New York Giants took on the Dallas Cowboys, receiver Amani Toomer of the Giants got some rough treatment by cornerback Aaron Hall of the cowboys. When Toomer finally snapped, and decked Hall while running a route, the referee threw his flag and called pass interference on Toomer. Toomer argued that Hall had been harassing him all game, and he was right; however, since the ref only saw Toomer's push (which had, without a doubt, been purposeful contact), he was justified and correct in throwing the flag. Now Toomer's argument did indeed have just as much merit, but since the ref hadn't seen the acts which he spoke of, the only truth he knew was that Toomer had committed a foul.

Conclusion fully addresses the complexities of the essay assignment.

Some things in life have absolute truth: the Knicks lost the game; Bush won the election. However, most areas of life are subject to interpretation and point of view: the Yankees are a good team; the Iraq war was justified, etc. Thus, truth really does depend (for the most part) on the person trying to decipher it. We see this from politics to sports, yet it is an idea that is truly had for people to grasp.

Excellent parallelism and repetition of sentence structure.

ESSAY 4: Traditional Essay

PROMPT: *"Does the truth change depending on perspective?"*

CORE TOPIC: Truth

Begins with a one-word sentence to entice the reader.

Perspective. Everyone has a different one, and they are how we see ourselves and the world around us. But is it more than just a way of seeing something? Perspective can change and distort our opinions, cause us to confuse truths, and falsehoods, or simply just interpret events differently. Every one has a unique point of view, allowing for different interpretations of truth.

Good thought-provoking question.

Clear thesis.

Awkward sentence structures throughout.

No book represents the different truths brought on by perspective greater than <u>To Kill a Mockingbird</u> by Harper Lee. In the racist southern town of Maycomb, Alabama, a boy named Jem Finch's father Atticus, takes up a court case defending a black man. For this, Jem and his family face much ridicule from many of Maycomb's residents. One woman in particular, Mrs. Dubose, throws especially caustic remarks at Jem whenever he walks by her house. Jem simply see this woman as old, senile, and cruel. And in many ways this is true. And, yet, Atticus sees her differently. Mrs. Dubose is a recovering morphine addict, and in Atticus' mind the truth is that she is a strong woman for trying to break free from substance abuse before she dies. Although both Jem and Atticus have opinions that are true, they differ because Atticus tried to look at the situation from the perspective of another and not through simply his own. This change in point of view allowed Atticus to see the whole picture and create an unbiased opinion.

Good transition.

While in this situation Atticus' truth was clearly better formulated and more thoughtful, in other situations it can be impossible to come to a "correct" conclusion. One strong example of this is the bombing of Hiroshima and Nagasaki by the USA near the end of World War II. Many feel that President Truman's decision to bomb these cities saved many American lives and put an end to a devastating war. Other, however, see it as a cruel human rights abuse that harmed civilians more than the military. Neither of these views on the truth can be called right or wrong. Each side

Strong historical example.

is equally passionate on their opinions and have evidence to back them up. Our world is not simply mathematics in which there is just one answer and everyone can tell if it is right or wrong. Atticus and Jem each had true beliefs but saw them from the perspective of others, while each side of the atom bomb debate argues over a possible different future that can never be understood. In most cases, there is no right way to look at something. In other words, "truth, like beauty, may lie in the eye of the beholder."

Ends with the quote but lacks a formal conclusion.

ESSAY 1: Loose Traditional Structure

PROMPT: *"Do changes that make our lives easier necessarily make them better?"*

CORE TOPIC: Technology

Beginning with an anecdote draws the reader in.

I once bought a silver bracelet that had a very interesting engraving. It read "I want to be/forever the me/ that greets change with open arms and heart." I found it inspirational, motivating and optimistic. However, I couldn't help myself from pondering the question: is change always better? Consider, if you will, the concept of "technology." Technological advancements can make our lives easier, no doubt.

Clearly stated thesis but not placed properly within the paragraph.

But just because some aspects of life get easier doesn't necessarily mean that life, overall, is better. Prior to the Scientific Revolution in mid-seventeenth century Europe, the average person was content. Scientific knowledge was based on the ancient ideas of the scholars and institutions, such as Aristotle, Ptolemy and the "all-knowing" Catholic Church. It came as a surprise, therefore, when Copernicus, in 1643, claimed that the Earth was not, after all, the center of the universe.

Concrete details!

From this one claim spiraled an infinite number of new proposals, the quest for new knowledge taking off at full speed, as technological advance usually does. A series of scientists developed theories about the placement of earth in the universe, the revolving patterns on the planets, and even went as far as to rethink the role of God in the whole mess of it all. People were astonished. True, scholars were thrilled. The mathematical proof confirmed all of their assumptions regarding natural law. True, these discoveries acted as the foundation for the discoveries that would rapidly unfold in the future. But what about those who did not take pleasure in these newfound claims?

Good thought-provoking questions.

What about the average European, who, not educated enough to understand, felt threatened? There had been a sense of security in knowing that there was a distinct "heaven and earth", in knowing that everything revolved around humans and their planet. The average person was scared. The average person was insecure. The average person felt as if they no longer had a purpose. The average

Stylistic repetition of "the average" demonstrates sophistication.

(cont.) *Stylistic repetition of "the average" demonstrates sophistication.*

person, despite the excitement aroused by scientific discoveries, wanted life to go back to the reliable way it had always been.

The one thing about change, I've realized, is that it is permanent. Once the first domino topples, the rest of the chain is bound to collapse. There is no turning back. Anyone in present society can see that technology has no termination, no destination, and no final point at which the world steps back and says, "Alright. We're done progressing." The idea of progress is embedded into human nature: the subconscious drive for man to push himself, challenging the accepted and paving new road.

Conclusion broadens the essay and brings it to the now.

Certainly, the advancements can be beneficial. Examine the current debate over the newly developed ability to choose the sex of an unborn child. On one hand, it makes life easier for parents who have a preference for one gender or the other. But with every advance in modern society comes the troubling question: is there a right or a wrong? Are these changes—stem cell research, cloning, even abortion—subject to ethical debate? Though advances made in technology, both during the Scientific Revolution and in modern society, may make life easier, it is clear at times they do not make life better.

ESSAY 2: Sandwich Structure

PROMPT: *"Do changes that make our lives easier necessarily make them better?"*

CORE TOPIC: Technology

Beginning with a narrative effectively draws the reader into the essay.

Descriptive language and details illustrate the essay's thesis.

There it was again, the quiet yet distinct sound that vibrated in the corner of my jacket pocket and disrupted what had been a jovial conversation between my dad and me. My dad peered down at my jacket for the third time in twenty minutes, his eyes and facial expression indicating a clear sense of irritation. It was a text message, the thing that bothered him most. And what was worse was the interruption it was becoming on our date together, a rare occasion in which we were finally hoping to take a break from all the chaos and noise of our hectic, jam-packed lives in order to simply enjoy each others company. But with my Motorola razor secured safely in my pocket, it became evident quite quickly that we had a third party on our date that night—a guest who my dad had not invited along but who I had consciously brought. The presence of my cell phone meant that throughout the night, I would remain connected to my friends, issues and my outside world. And as for my dad? Well, he would just have to get used to it.

Good transition.

In today's world, society is constantly being bombarded with new forms of technology such as more efficient mean of communication (for me, the razor was the communication means of choice). Laptops, ipods, blackberries, and cell phones are among the hundreds of devices that have filtrated through communities across the globe in order to make life easier. In a recent article in Time magazine pertaining to technology, researchers pointed out that more people are able to multi-task than ever before. More children spend hours connected to high-speed Internet than ever before. More way of interconnecting people and ideas (at the fastest rate possible) are present than ever before. And sure—all of these devices make my life easier. But it's also necessary to question whether or not these changes and technological conveniences are really making our lives better or enriched. To be enriched would be to have more pleasurable contacts, happier

Current events impact the reader.

relationships, and a fulfilling life "beyond the screen" as it states in Time.

Returns to the original narrative and adheres to the sandwich structure. Conclusion fully addresses the essay assignment.

As I sat at the restaurant with my dad, he looked more hurt by my lack of attention to him than content that my communication with my friends was "better." Similarly, as millions of parents across the globe witness a sharp decrease in the amount of family dinners or interactive activities they participate in, I doubt that they consider themselves happier. Easier does not mean more enriched, and therefore the advancements in technology that make our lives easier do not necessarily make them better.

ESSAY 3: Traditional Structure

PROMPT: *"Do changes that make our lives easier necessarily make them better?"*

CORE TOPIC: Technology

Including strong details in the introduction lures the reader.

In the 18th century, Eli Whitney invented interchangeable parts. The purpose of these parts was to make repairs easier. If one part broke, one could just buy the equivalent part, without having to reconstruct the entire item. Interchangeable parts had an important effect on guns. Instead of having to fix guns by hand, a long and tedious process, one could just replace them. This dramatically increased the production and selling of guns. In the Civil War, millions died because guns were more easily accessible than in Revolutionary time. Although this shows that changes that make our lives easier don't necessarily make them better, it was only the beginning.

Good transition.

Excellent body examples but lacking detail and development.

As time progressed, more and more advancements were made in war technology. Eventually many different kinds of guns were manufactured along with tanks and, later on, aircrafts. While these machines would prove useful in combat, how can one argue that killing people makes our lives better? In World War I, millions were killed because of advanced machinery. Trench warfare between France and Germany became a war of attrition; in other words, the side that lost too many men first would have to give up. Even so, about a quarter of a century later, technology threatened our lives to a far greater extent.

Working with a team of scientists, Albert Einstein developed the atomic (or nuclear) bomb. While at the time (World War II), this seemed beneficial for the United States, but in later times it would instill a great fear in us. Dropping the atomic bomb on Hiroshima and Nagasaki in Japan killed millions. Though we weren't concerned with a nuclear response because they were incapable of producing one, more recent years have given us reason to be afraid.

During the Cold War, the Cuban Missile Crisis almost resulted in an all-out nuclear war, which would have definitely proven that changes that make our life easier don't necessarily make life better. Although the crisis

(cont.) *Excellent body examples but lacking detail and development.*

was narrowly avoided, there would be more to come. Recently, the U.S. Government feared that Iraq was housing weapons of "mass destruction". President Bush insisted on investigating. Later, it was discovered that no such weapons existed. However, the possibility that they did exist created a fear in the American public. How can something that scares us so much make our lives better? Even today, the government is intent on invading other Middle Eastern countries to try to discover their nuclear weapons. Our invasion of these countries gives us reason to be afraid that they my attack us, possibly ending some of our lives.

Conclusion addresses and refutes the opposition.

One cannot argue that being killed by nuclear warfare makes one's life better. While certain elements of advancement in technology have certainly helped make aspects of life easier, it is clear that not all of this progress has made our lives better. We can only hope that in the future we can try to make changes that won't have us questioning whether or not our lives are in jeopardy.

ESSAY 4: Sandwich Structure

PROMPT: *"Do changes that make our lives easier necessarily make them better?"*

CORE TOPIC: Technology

Opens with an anecdote that leads a reader to the thesis.

I opened up the bright wrapping paper to my big 13th Birthday present, a cell phone. Extremely excited, I peeled off the plastic cover and immediately began to put all my friends numbers into my phone. I could talk to my friends whenever I wanted to! With the onset of my new phone came an abundance of funny text messages, pictures, and bothersome phone calls. With the new freedom and fun of a cell phone also came the superfluous calls from home, on feeding the dog, when to come home and what to do. Although my cell phone made finding friends and rides easier, it also made my life more tiresome with so many reprimanding, reminding phone calls from my parents. Has this made my life better?

Good questioning here.

Too much plot summary.

New technology is introduced every day, but does it really help us live better lives? "The Veldt" a short story by Ray Bradbury, examines the role of the rise of technology in family life. Wendy and Peter grow up in a house that does it all; it cooks, cleans, and cares for the children. It also provides entertainment in the form of the nursery. The nursery is a room that transforms into whatever the children wish for. The parents recognize their children's reliance on technology and turn off the nursery. However, by this point in their lives, the children are so detached emotionally and physically from their parents that they wholeheartedly hate them for this action. The nursery reflects this hate and the parents are destroyed by it. While the technologically advanced house made the family's lives easier, it eventually destroyed the family unit.

Good transition.

In my own family, our lives are consumed by new technology, With the ring of the telephone, and constant buzz of the television, conversations are held through text messages, dinners are interrupted by phone calls, and watching movies replaces playing games. I begin to wonder if all that's supposed to improve our lives is actually doing the opposite.

ESSAY 1: Narrative Structure

PROMPT: *"Perfection is not interesting; it is the flaws that fascinate."*

CORE TOPIC: Perfection

Dialogue immediately hooks the reader.

"Gosh Rachel, what is that?" my friend Beth asked me. Suddenly, a crowd of students from my photography class were huddled around my latest photo.

Strong parallel sentence structure. Illustrative language helps to show rather than tell.

My face turned a deep shade of crimson. In my mind, I thought my photograph was perfectly acceptable and followed the instructions of the assignment. As each of my perplexed classmates poked and examined my photo, my mind was filled with doubts and fears. This was the most important project of the semester. If I did not follow through with the requirements, I would be doomed. It was clear that my peers agreed with my worst fear: they could not understand my subject choice, my lighting choice or my lens choice.

Just as butterflies in my stomach were about to explode from my abdomen because of my nervousness, my photography teacher entered, Ms. Brady. Now my nerves really started to kick in. Ms. Brady was notorious for her strictness and provincial thinking. She slowly walked around the room, examining each piece. When she stopped at my piece, Ms. Brady's eyes widened. Immediately, she grabbed my arm and told me that the picture was too dark, certain sections were too blurry and I had used the wrong lens. My fate had been sealed—or so I thought.

Good transition.

Ms. Brady's face lit up with a smile. She explained that the flaws of my photograph were what captured the attention of the class and herself. If I had followed the assignment exactly, I would not have captured photography's imperfectness and beauty.

Not a real word.

By stepping out of the box, I was able to try something new and capture attention. After class, even Beth congratulated me on my pictures. Sometimes mistakes are right: "nothing perfect is interesting; it is the flaws that fascinate."

Ends narrative with direct quotation of essay prompt.

ESSAY 2: Traditional Essay
PROMPT: *"Perfection is not interesting; it is the flaws that fascinate."*
CORE TOPIC: Perfection

Beauty lies everywhere around us. It is the sound of the birds singing outside. It is the funny smell of your garage. But why do we find these things beautiful? The reason for this lies in the fact that we find beauty in things that interest us. But without imperfection, nothing would be interesting. Perfect things do not catch our eyes; they are plain and boring. But it is the flaws that truly ignite our excitement, and flaws that make things stick in our memoires.

Not a logical example of beauty.

Clear thesis.

An example of this can be found in the film Pleasantville. Prior to when outsiders from the real world arrive, Pleasantville is "perfect." Nothing ever goes wrong, beside perhaps a cat getting stuck in a tree, and everyone is fairly content. But when real people arrive, they bring along with them not only new customs and ideas, but also emotions. And when this begins to spread around town, it creates quite an uproar. Some are afraid of the change— things beginning to have color, and kids beginning to listen to rock and roll and to have sex. The whole of the town is uneasy and very close minded. But in the end, emotions begin to spread to everyone, and soon the whole town is colored and beautiful. So although certain "bad" elements of the real world were introduced, people in the town learned to love and have emotions—truly a beautiful, but not perfect thing.

Excellent detail.

Another example can be seen in Edward Albee's American Dream. In this play, he portrays the American Dream of perfection as not so perfect at all. Parents in the play chose a "perfect" child, but in fact he has no feelings or emotions. He is so "perfect," that he is not even human, but more of a machine.

Good transition but fails to restate the main idea..

Poor development.

So it is in the flaws where beauty truly lies. "Nothing perfect is interesting, it is the flaws that fascinate." Perhaps our search for perfection is not so admirable. Perhaps we look to better ourselves in all the wrong places. So we must ask ourselves, do we really want to be "perfect" if perfect means nothing more than plain and insipid?

Great detail but awkwardly worded.

Vocab!

ESSAY 3: Narrative Structure

PROMPT: *"Perfection is not interesting; it is the flaws that fascinate."*

CORE TOPIC: Perfection

Excellent parallelism.

Models. Movie stars. Glamorous people. Flawless people. The average Joe and Jane envy the people they see in the movies, on the television screen; the people they will never meet and never become. Everyone has been an average Joe or Jane at least one time in his or her life. It is easy to envy these people we see on television because they are projected to be perfect. Because we never see the flaws, we just assume they don't exist. But there is no such thing as perfection. Everyone has flaws.

Clear thesis but no introduction of topics.

Lots of details help elucidate the narrative, but too many details can be overwhelming—readers lose track of the thesis here.

Since as far back as I can remember, people have always thought of me as perfect. To the outside eye, my life might in fact seem perfect. I get good grades; I am a good athlete; I am a good artist . . . etc. However, there are a lot of things that people don't know about me. People don't know these things because I don't tell them. I don't share my imperfections with my peers because I can't let them think I'm not perfect.

Keeping all of my flaws secrets keep me aloof from the rest of my peers. I never feel attached to anyone nor do they feel attached to me, because they know and I know that I keep things from them. For example, I just turned sixteen in June. When December rolled around, I knew that I had to pass my road test. There was no excuse for not passing; I had to be perfect. All of the pressure mounted up, and when the test finally came, I failed. "What? No! This can't be! I can't fail! I'm . . . well, I'm me!" Thoughts like these raced through my head when I thought about what I would tell everyone. I had kept the date a secret for fear that I would fail, but I never thought it would actually happen. "No! I can't tell anyone! I won't be perfect anymore. I can't."

So, I told no one about my failure and let everyone keep believing that I was flawless. When the date for my make-up test came, I had even more pressure on my back. I had failed one—I could fail again. But, buckling under

(cont.) Lots of details help elucidate the narrative, but too many details can be overwhelming— readers lose track of the thesis here.

the pressure yet again, I failed another time. "How could this be? Was my perfection slipping away? No! I can't let anyone know. If no one knows, I can still be perfect!"

I wiped the tears from my eyes—yes, I was crying—and decided, again, not to tell anyone. However, people were getting suspicious. My coach had told my basketball team that I had my road test (I was forced to tell him to get out of practice to go take the test), and they all asked me if I had passed at the next practice. I told them I failed, and with tears in my eyes, I tried to explain what happened. I told them excuses and how it was unfair, and blah blah blah.

I felt horrible—like I had let everyone down! Just as I thought all hope was lost, one of my teammates called me. She told me about how at least half of her friends failed their road tests a couple of times before they passed. Another one of my friends told me about how she was reassured that I wasn't as perfect as she thought.

Maybe, people weren't meant to be perfect. Maybe, the flaws are what keep things real. Maybe, the flaws are necessary. I'm not perfect. I have my flaws, just like everyone else. Those movie stars and models on television aren't perfect either. They all have faults, and these faults are what make them who they are. "Perfection is not always what it seems; the flaws are more interesting."

Excellent link back to the opening paragraph.

Ends with the direct quote!

ESSAY 4: Narrative Structure
PROMPT: *"Perfection is not interesting; it is the flaws that fascinate."*
CORE TOPIC: Perfection

Jumps right into the narrative and grabs the reader's attention.

I sighed loudly as I folded the wrinkled copy of "The Patent Trader" and slammed it on the kitchen table. Yet again, the reporters had written about Morgan, John Jay's soccer sensation that I simply despised. Over and over her accomplishments and her zillions of goals had been written about; over and over had her team been given this perfect, flawless image. Quite simply, this was old news.

Excellent details that address the essay question.

Thought-provoking question!

What about my high school team? We had just gone through a rough transition from the spring season into the fall, leaving our squad with holes where players used to fill, but had chosen to play another fall sport instead. Our coach was a stranger; our assistant, almost mute. Our captain? One had quit during pre-season, the other was out of shape with a sprained ankle. We were a mess. But still, we had managed to come together, found leadership in foreign places, and had a great time. Most importantly, we shut down the so-called "perfect" Morgan and defeated the "flawless" John Jay's team in a 1-0 victory to win the section.

In the end, it didn't matter that John Jay had beaten our team 2-0 and 4-0 during the season. They come into the section championship game cocky, while we were playing our hearts out with nothing to lose. Yet it seemed that nothing good can last forever. We lost a windy, unfortunate game in the state quarter-finals, but we had a great run. At our last team dinner our parents gossiped and laughed together. My teammate and I chatted excitedly about the next season and our coach, now a great friend, proudly held up the front page of the "The Patent Trader" and read us the headline: "John Jay falls to the Mighty G-Force." The article was the paper's main focus, picking apart every one of our successes to reveal the pain and drama that lay underneath. True, John Jay had a small write-up next to our article, but it merely noted their success and congratulated the seniors. It

Beautiful sentence variety.

(cont.) Beautiful sentence variety. seemed everyone, especially my team, was sick of reading about the same perfect tale, because really "nothing perfect is interesting; it's the flaws that fascinate." Though we had our flaws, they only made our team's success look all the greater-once again, we had won.

Includes a direct quotation of the essay prompt.

ESSAY 5: Sandwich Structure

PROMPT: *"Perfection is not interesting; it is the flaws that fascinate."*

CORE TOPIC: Perfection

This paragraph starts off with engaging and descriptive language but ends abruptly without providing a clear thesis.

His ragged body lays upon my bed. The ghosts of eyes stare into the distance. Age wrinkles are replaced by bare spots of fur. The nose, once a pink glossy pebble, is now an empty hole. The pink, plush, and fluffy body is now old, gray, and ratty. The stuffing spills out of various holes. This is my teddy bear, Teddy. He may not seem like the typical stuffed animal, and this is true. He is much more special.

Missing transition.

Joan of Arc is now a Saint, and people thought she was perfect. She helped France in their war against England and led them to many victories. It was the flaws that made her interesting. She dressed like a man, fought in battles, and argued with kings. However, she was burned at the stake and accused of witchcraft. All of this makes her very interesting.

Very superficial; minimal detail is provided.

Teddy has lived much more than many other stuffed animals have. He has traveled the "world," Teddy has been to the Bronx Zoo, Central Park, McDonald's, nursery school; just about anywhere a three year old little girl would have gone. He has also gone through a lot of tragedy in his life. Teddy has lost his nose and both of his eyes, because of a mishap with my dog. Teddy has gone through a lot for a bear of sixteen years old. Although Teddy may not be perfect, he is very special. Every part of him tells a story. He has seen a lot that is while he still had eyes. His flaws just show how his life has been one of adventure and experience. Teddy may have stuffing coming out at all sides, but along with the stuffing, comes fascinating stories.

Does not fully address why flaws are fascinating.

ANSWER KEY FOR SAMPLE ESSAYS

COOPERATION ESSAY 1

SCORE: 9

This essay used strong examples to support a clearly defined thesis and provided adequate detail in the body paragraphs. More detail is needed to push this essay to a higher level—especially from the book *To Kill A Mockingbird*. Specific events from the novel are not incorporated, and the essay lost a point here. The additional point deductions were a result of missing transitions that took away from the essay's cohesion and from the undefined term in the introduction. The essay states that success has different meanings, but fails to qualify this statement by defining success as it will be developed in the essay. Always define the vague terms used in the essay prompt.

COOPERATION ESSAY 2

SCORE: 11

This well-written essay thoroughly details examples in support of a clear, well-defined thesis. Transitions fluidly connect ideas, sentence structure is varied, and vocabulary is consistently strong. This essay lost a point in the introduction. The wording is awkward and a reader must fumble through some redundancy before the thesis is presented. The conclusion is also cumbersome and should be broken into shorter sentences that present concise ideas.

COOPERATION ESSAY 3

SCORE: 10

This competent essay starts and ends strongly with detailed and interesting examples presented in both the introduction and conclusion. Vocabulary is strong throughout. The historical examples are adequately detailed, providing support for a clear and focused thesis. This essay lost points because there is no transition leading to the final paragraph about Nephel. This paragraph, although the final paragraph of the essay, reads like a body paragraph and does not fully conclude the essay. Summation of the Galileo and Dubois examples needs to be included to provide more concrete closure.

COOPERATION ESSAY 4

SCORE: 8

This adequate essay effectively focuses a reader on a clear thesis. Dialogue and narrative are used to lure and engage readers at the start of the essay, but the "trap" quickly dissipates. This essay lost points because it is vague and general and lacks the needed detail to make the essay interesting. The writer does bring up and rebut the opposition, an effective technique in persuasive writing. However, the rebuttal is, like the entire essay, lacking detail and concrete examples. This essay would have scored much higher had the writer used the sandwich structure. The introduction should have been the narrative, the body a more concrete example, and the conclusion should have revisited the narrative.

COOPERATION ESSAY 5
SCORE: 12
This exemplary traditional essay adheres strictly to proper form and organization. The introduction provides the reader with a clear thesis and topics to come. Body paragraphs focus the reader on the thesis while providing ample detail and development. Transitions link both supporting examples so that reading is effortless. The conclusion restates the thesis and main points of the essay, as well as broadens to encompass modern day. Mentioning current events in an essay is an excellent way to impact the reader.

TRUTH ESSAY 1
SCORE: 10
This competent essay develops history and literature to fully address the essay prompt. Truth and perspective are clearly defined; a strong thesis is presented in the introduction; vocabulary is strong throughout. This essay lost points because of weak topic sentences and transitions. There is no sentence linking the middle two body paragraphs, and the essay jumps from the American Revolution to *Of Mice and Men*.

TRUTH ESSAY 2
SCORE: 11
This detailed, persuasive essay is organized, focused, and well supported with detailed and developed examples. Strong transitions allow readers to easily move from one body paragraph to the next. The examples in each body paragraph indicate the writer's full understanding of the essay prompt. The writer fully develops his point with clear, detailed specifics taken from *1984*. Plot summary is avoided, taking the paragraph beyond a level of superficiality to a more engaging, mature level. The essay lost a point because it does not provide a clear thesis in the introduction. All traditionally structured essays should have an introductory thesis statement so that readers are prepared to follow the direction the essay will take.

TRUTH ESSAY 3
SCORE: 12
This exemplary essay addresses and analyzes the essay prompt to the fullest degree. The essay uses several current event details to entice readers and lead them to more developed body paragraphs that further support the writer's thesis. Transitional sentences give the essay fluidity, so that a reader may glide through each paragraph seamlessly. Consistent sentence variety, rhetorical questioning, and parallelism make the essay engaging throughout.

TRUTH ESSAY 4

SCORE: 9

This capable essay has a clear thesis, strong transitional sentences, and a focused conclusion. The body paragraphs contain adequate supporting details, but the sentence structure within those paragraphs does not demonstrate a mastery of writing. The paragraph about *To Kill a Mockingbird*, although detailed, develops too much plot summary. Additionally, the second body paragraph lacks specificity; WWII and the bombing of Hiroshima should be further investigated in this paragraph.

TECHNOLOGY ESSAY 1

SCORE: 11

This competent essay fully addresses the essay question. Clear definitions of terms are presented, creating a set of parameters for the reader. Rhetorical questioning is used to push the essay to a more engaging level. Supporting evidence is slightly undeveloped, and although the writer points to the Scientific Revolution and the Catholic Church as evidence that technology does not make life better, he fails to provide enriching, concrete specifics. The essay does have a high intellectual and philosophical aspect to it, but philosophical musings do not entirely replace hard evidence. Therefore, although the writing is highly sophisticated, this essay lost points because it lacked specific details.

TECHNOLOGY ESSAY 2

SCORE: 12

This narrative beautifully and fully examines the essay prompt. Vivid detail creates a picture for the reader and makes the essay more engaging. Strong transitions make the story flawlessly coherent, and the essay's conclusion broadens the narrative to reach a wider audience. A clear and focused thesis is provided in the last sentence of the essay—the narrative is used to "prove" this thesis correct.

TECHNOLOGY ESSAY 3

SCORE: 10

This essay is packed full of examples used to support the writer's position. The breadth of supporting examples is impressive, but due to the fact that there are only twenty-five minutes to contrast the essay, the writer did not have adequate time to fully develop all of his supporting examples. Traditionally structured essays should draw upon two examples and develop, detail, and analyze how these two examples relate to the essay prompt. The essay lost its second point because of underdeveloped ideas presented in the body paragraphs.

TECHNOLOGY ESSAY 4

SCORE: 9

This essay starts off strong with a descriptive narrative. It returns to this narrative in the end, creating a cohesive sandwich essay. However, a transition from the narrative to the short story is missing. Also, the body paragraphs provide too much plot summary and not enough concrete detail. Therefore, this essay is only adequately developed and illustrates only a general understanding of the essay prompt.

PERFECTION ESSAY 1

SCORE: 11

This strong essay beautifully develops the fascination of flaws through a detailed and focused narrative. The dialogue is used effectively to draw a reader into the story. The details, essay structure, and vocabulary all demonstrate the author's maturity as a writer. This essay scored an 11 rather than a 12 because, sadly, College Board evaluates essay length. Unfortunately, this essay is rather short. There are also some slightly awkwardly worded sentences.

PERFECTION ESSAY 2

SCORE: 8

This essay could have been strong and persuasive, but the introduction neither fully addresses nor prepares the reader for the argument presented in the body paragraphs. The topic sentences are weak—they do represent a map of the main points addressed in the essay. The paragraph about the film has wonderful detail, but a movie is not a good example that should be used in support of a thesis. In comparison to the *Pleasantville* paragraph, the American dream paragraph is severely underdeveloped and lacks adequate detail. As a whole, the essay is cohesive, organized, and presents a logical argument, using two separate and relevant examples. Therefore, the essay is "adequate" and received a score of 8.

PERFECTION ESSAY 3

SCORE: 10

This solid essay clearly addressed the essay question with focus and detail. The essay lost points because of the third and fourth paragraphs. These paragraphs dragged and contained too much dialogue and too many rhetorical questions. Paragraphs should lead directly to the thesis, found in the sixth body paragraph. The essay lost additional points because the essay question was not addressed in its entirety. The prompt asks if it is the flaws that fascinate—this essay failed to fully address the fascination component of the essay question.

PERFECTION ESSAY 4

SCORE: 12

This stellar essay is organized, coherent, and concise. The narrative effectively lures a reader in by use of dialogue, rhetorical questioning, and imagery. The details provided lead and focus the reader on the author's thesis, which clearly addresses the essay prompt. But be careful: this essay shines because the writer is eloquent. Most essays about sports—a trying moment, a disappointment, a win at the last minute—sound cliché and flat. We recommend that students do not write about their team sports unless the student is an extremely strong writer.

PERFECTION ESSAY 5

SCORE: 7

This underdeveloped essay fails to fully address the essay prompt. The narrative, although structurally organized and clearly written, does not present enough detail to demonstrate the author's complete understanding of the issue. The conclusion is vague, inadequately addressing why it is that flaws are fascinating.

CHAPTER 14

INTRODUCING THE ACT ESSAY: THIRTY MINUTES OF PERSUASION

The ACT is another standardized test option for college-bound students. All colleges and universities will accept ACT scores in place of SAT scores and vice versa.

The ACT offers an optional writing component to students registering for the exam.

However—though the idea of spending an additional thirty minutes composing an essay after an already arduous three hours of Scantron bubbling may not be appealing—we strongly recommend that students register for this test with the writing component.

We strongly recommend that students register for the ACT with writing.

This is because many colleges will not accept ACT scores without a writing component score. Therefore, don't limit yourself with college choices—opt to sit for the essay. Besides, with a little practice, the essay becomes the easiest part of the test.

The ACT and the SAT are alike in that both essays are graded by two graders who can give from 1-6 points. These two scores are added together, with a perfect essay scoring a total of 12 points. Unlike the SAT essay, the ACT essay score does not affect the overall composite ACT score. Rather, it is presented as its own score, out of 12. An average essay score is a 6. You should be shooting for well above average—a 9 to 12.

Attaining this above-average ACT score is easy. With the tips provided in this chapter (and many that you'll utilize from the previous SAT chapters) you'll be able to prove your point and persuade the reader in only thirty minutes.

The ACT Challenge

Unlike the SAT essay assignment, the ACT essay assignment does not easily relate to history or literature. Instead, the ACT essay prompt briefly describes a current, "controversial" issue that you will very probably be able to relate to easily. Issues such as the controversy of high-school locker searches, dating, uniforms, and the thought of year-round school are not quite comparable to heroes who sacrificed their lives or presidents who made sweeping changes.

You must pick a side and prove this side to be correct.

You'll be relying on your own personal experience to provide the details for an ACT essay. These details (either real or made up) must be used to support and develop your broad statements. Despite the differences between the essay topics, however, you will still be responsible for writing clearly and well.

The ACT essay presents you with the issue and two opposing viewpoints. Of course, there's always room for compromise, but not in thirty minutes and not in this essay. You must take a stance on the issue presented and persuade the reader to see things your way. There is no "straddling the fence." Choose a side!

The following is a standard ACT essay prompt.

In some high schools, many teachers and parents have encouraged the school to adopt a dress code that sets guidelines for what students can wear in the school building. Some teachers and parents support a dress code because they think it will improve the learning environment in the school. Other teachers and parents do not support a dress code because they think it restricts the individual student's freedom of expression. In your opinion, should high schools adopt dress codes for students?

"In your essay, take a position on this question. You may write about either one of the two points of view given, or you may present a different point of view on this question. Use specific reasons and examples to support your position."

The response will be evaluated on your ability to:

• maintain focus throughout the essay
• develop a position by using logical reasoning
• support your ideas with specific examples
• organize your essay in a cohesive manner
• use appropriate language effectively

Sounds easy, right? There's a slight catch. The prompt often revolves around an issue that is relevant to high-school students (dress codes, community service, extracurricular activities, etc.). As these are high-school related issues, you may have very partisan viewpoints on the issue you are writing about. However, this can work against you!

Issues that deeply affect you typically elicit strong opinions. However, writing a subjective and biased opinion is hardly persuasive. The goal is to avoid unsupported, opinionated writing and to rely on factual, detailed, objective writing to compose a compelling ACT persuasive essay in thirty minutes.

Build your argument on facts; don't merely express unsupported opinions.

Build a Winning Argument

Imagine the essay as a verbal argument. You've all had one of those. Think of the last time Mom wouldn't let you go out: a battle till the end! When asked to give one reason why she should let you go out, you pause before stammering, "Because I want to!" *Real convincing.* Had you anticipated this question and been prepared with an answer, you might be walking out that door to a fun party. But instead, you're stuck at home with an angry mom.

The ACT presents a similar problem. If you just dive into the essay unprepared, reason is eclipsed by emotion. Therefore, spend five minutes outlining your essay, the major points of the argument, and think about possible rebuttals to opposing views. (And keep in mind, next time you want to ask to go out, to borrow the car, or to miss your sister's ballet recital, prepare your argument ahead of time!)

The following steps detail your plan of attack. Spend a full five minutes preparing and outlining your argument. You have the time, so use it to really prepare and organize.

STEP 1: GENERATE PROS AND CONS

After reading the essay prompt, circle the key words within the question. Construct a pro/con chart in the margin of your paper. List all the possible benefits of the situation, and all the possible negatives. Be creative! The issue will have some bearing on you as a teenager, so put yourself in the situation described. What would you like? What would you not like?

You have a full five minutes to plan your response (coming up with ideas, organizing your points, creating a basic outline). Don't rush! Spend the time and be as creative as possible. Generate "outside the box" pros and cons. Everyone will develop the obvious. You need to develop the *less obvious.* Creative responses will stand out—set your essay apart and push your score from average to awesome.

The following is a sample pro/con chart in response to: *"Should high-school students be required to wear school uniforms?"*

> Spend five minutes preparing and outlining your argument.

Pros	Cons
• less "judging" by peers	• waste of money
• less time getting ready in the morning	• ugly/unflattering
• less distraction in the classroom	• eliminates individuality
• prepares students for work force	

STEP 2: CHOOSE YOUR SIDE

After constructing a quick pro/con chart, choose your side. Now, before choosing, remember that your personal opinion does not matter. Your feelings do not matter. In fact, not to burst your bubble of self-esteem, *you* do not matter in this essay. All that matters is your ability to develop the argument and persuade, through logic and substance, the reader. Therefore, choose the side you can write more about! Disregard personal opinion and opt to write about the bulkier side of your outline—pro or con. Even if it's the side you don't believe in, you should choose the side you have more to write about. This will be the *easier* side. Easy is good!

STEP 3: PLAN YOUR ATTACK

You've brainstormed. You've outlined. And now, you're about to write your essay. But, choose your words wisely—persuasion is an art. Through your writing, you must get into the reader's head and control his or her thoughts. Creepy, yes. But it's also a manageable feat. Simply present your argument in a logical manner: Start with a broad, general statement. Then, funnel the reader down your path of thinking by qualifying these broad statements with one or two concrete specifics—use details! Again, just as you could embellish or completely make up personal details for the SAT essay, you can embellish like crazy on the ACT. These details (both the real and the fictional) will support and develop your broad statements.

Note: Refer to the other chapters in this book for tips about beginning your essay, developing points, using transitions, meeting/rebutting your opposition, and ending the essay well.

STEP 4: SHOOT DOWN THE OPPOSITION

Once you've chosen a side, you've simultaneously chosen "the enemy." In order to truly persuade the reader and validate your decision, you must shoot down this enemy—the other side. Select one reason you came up with from the opposite side. Think of an example that contradicts this point. In proving the other side wrong, you're proving yourself correct.

So, next time Mom points out that you can't go out because you forgot to take out the garbage, be prepared with a strong, creative rebuttal.

> *Yes, Mom, I see your point. But, although being punished for my irresponsibility is understandable, by allowing me to go out tonight, you'll be motivating me to complete my chores in the future.*

This is much more convincing than jumping up and down and screaming that nothing in life is fair!

Notice the subtly of the counter-argument: *Yes, I see your point. But, this is why it's incorrect.* Eliminate subjective tones and assertively state your arguments as facts. There is no "I think," "In my opinion," or "I believe" in this persuasive essay. Everything should be stated as if it applies to all and as if there is no doubt in your mind that you are correct in saying so.

Now it's your turn. Create two outline charts like the one on the next page. Come up with reasons that address the sample issues, anticipate the opposition's position, and shoot them down. Remember, be creative and try to come up with at least three distinct reasons either in support of or against the issue. Your sample topics:

1. *"Should students be allowed to drive to school or should they be required to ride the bus?"*
2. *"Should schools eliminate proms and other social events?"*

> *Don't say "I think," "In my opinion," or "I believe" in your essay.*

Pros	Cons
1.	1.
2.	2.
3.	3.
4.	4.
Position:	
Opposition:	
Rebuttal:	

The Seven Sins: Mistakes Students Make when Writing a Persuasive Essay

Now, in order to be as persuasive as possible, you must avoid the following common mistakes. These mistakes lead to loopholes in logic, counter-reasoning, and a failure to fully persuade. You'll find tips on how to avoid them throughout this book.

1. FORGETTING YOUR AUDIENCE

Let us remember, middle-aged, college-educated teachers are reading your essay. You want to impress them with sophisticated writing—sentence variety, vocabulary, and content. Try to write as maturely as possible, avoiding juvenile language such as "kids," "stuff," and "lots."

Watch your language! Remember your audience.

2. IGNORING THE HUMAN ELEMENT

As much as you'd like to think otherwise, essay graders are people, too. And, even though they're getting paid to read your essay, they can still get bored. Terribly bored at that. So, make sure to include "hooks" and "lures" to grab the reader's attention. Thought-provoking questions, personal anecdotes, and clear writing with details and specifics will appeal to the reader. I recommend beginning with a personal anecdote, one that illustrates and exemplifies your thesis.

3. LACKING SUPPORTING DETAILS

Remember when you were three years old and there was always a "why" attached to everything in life? Daddy is going to the store. Why? It's time for dinner. Why? Get in the car. Why? Don't hit your sister. Why? We're dealing with more profound issues than getting in a car and driving somewhere, but consider a reader like a giant, educated, experienced three-year-old.

Start with an anecdote.

Every statement you make should include an answer to that anticipated "why." You need to convince these teacher-toddlers that your statements are legitimate. Include supporting examples and details. Once again, don't be afraid to include details and evidence from your own experience!

4. CONFUSING FACTS WITH OPINIONS

Although the essay is opinion-based, it should read as factually as possible. Opinions without reasons are not convincing and can easily be knocked down. Cold, hard facts and valid examples, on the other hand, are indisputable, and they strengthen your essay.

For example:

> **OPINION:** Students deserve a year off after many strenuous years.
> **FACT:** By the time students graduate from high school, they have been in school for thirteen consecutive years, a massive percentage of their entire lives.

> **OPINION:** Students want to spend their free time doing fun stuff, not community service.

FACT: Between eight hours of sleep, nine hours in school, sports practice, drama rehearsal, working on the student magazine, homework, spending time with the family, and walking the dog, leisure time for a student can be in lamentably short supply.

5. BEING TOO EXTREME

Although you want to make the statements in your essay applicable to more than just you, you can't make them apply to everyone. Using extremes (all, always, never, nobody etc.) creates fallacies. Fallacies, or false statements, are over simplifications that require only one exception to be rendered incorrect and invalid. So, avoid the extremes. Rather, qualify answers with less general modifiers from the following list:

- a few
- a great deal
- a little bit
- a lot
- almost all
- customarily
- generally
- many
- most
- nearly
- occasionally
- often
- ordinarily
- sometimes
- usually

6. LACKING AN ORGANIZED ANSWER

You don't want your essay to read like a ping-pong match: one good thing about one side, one bad thing about another. Two more good things, one more bad thing, etc. Bouncing readers back and forth between pros, cons, for, against—they'll go cross-eyed. Cross-eyed readers will not give you a high mark on this exam! Therefore, present your argument in a logical, coherent, organized fashion. Start with a generalization, and then include specifics to qualify and support this general statement. Then, move on to another generalization, and include specifics that qualify your second, general point.

7. DISREGARDING THE OPPOSITION

Think about yourself. Once your mind is made up, it's very difficult to change it. No matter how much you're coaxed, bribed, or argued with, you cling to your original opinion. Like you, readers have an opinion, and not necessarily one that agrees with your own. Therefore, it'll take some work to convince them otherwise. Putting in the effort to change their opinions, though, is essential. You must bring in and subsequently disprove your opposition.

Transitions are crucial to the cohesiveness of your argument.

The last body paragraph of your essay should include the opposition and appropriate "shoot down" of this opposition. Shooting down the opposition is the last step involved in building your argument. In order to bring in the opposition, though, you'll need to include strong transitions. These transitions will allow you to gracefully move from one side of the argument to the other without confusing the reader. See more about transitions in Chapter 5.

Structure a Persuasive Response

The ACT essay is a traditional persuasive essay that lends itself nicely to the traditional essay structure (intro, body, body, conclusion) that is discussed in Chapter 4. However, don't be afraid to stray slightly from this structure. If you have a multitude of supporting examples, it may be best to have several body paragraphs.

INTRODUCTION: WHICH SIDE?

Introductions should be short and sweet. Tease the reader a bit with a "bang": a thought-provoking question, a one-word sentence, or a personal anecdote.

Beginning with a personal anecdote is my favorite way to start an ACT essay. It pulls the grader in and prevents you from "spilling the beans" and giving away all your supporting examples in the introduction. Make sure this narrative is succinct, directly relates to the essay question, and leads the reader to your position.

Note the following example written in response to the question: *"Should high school require students to wear uniforms?"*

> *Shannon Walters was wearing pink today. She sat three chairs over, and she looked really cute in pink. I have no idea what Pythagorean's theorem stated, but I do know that Shannon Walters was the cutest girl in my math class. Maybe Shannon wouldn't have been quite so distracting in a school uniform. In fact, all schools should choose to adopt dress codes to minimize distraction and maximize learning.*

Once again, your goal is to hook the reader with a catchy opening and to clearly state your position on the essay presented. Do not delve into your numerous reasons for choosing this side in the introduction—you'll ruin the surprise. Simply state your position as a thesis and force the reader to continue reading.

Last, if you do choose to grab the reader with a personal anecdote (as I recommend), be sure to follow up and revisit this anecdote in the conclusion.

BODY PARAGRAPH ONE: WHY THAT SIDE?

In the first body paragraph, clump together the reasons you came up with in support of your position. Do not name them off like a shopping list. Detail each reason. Provide examples that illustrate each point (and make the essay longer!). Sometimes, this body paragraph is best broken into two or three mini-paragraphs, depending upon your reasons, examples, and writing style.

Regardless, all reasons and examples in support of your position should be present up front and together. Bombard the readers with evidence. Overwhelm them with facts and details. Validate. Convince. Remember, you can include details about yourself to quantify any broad statements.

BODY PARAGRAPH TWO: WHY NOT THE OTHER SIDE?

You don't want to leave any room for second-guessing in this essay. Therefore, stay one step ahead of readers. Anticipate their doubts. Counter-argue. The second body paragraph should bring to light one or two points in support of the opposition. And then, *WHAM!* Shoot down this opposition. By proving the other side wrong, you are simultaneously proving yourself right. *Proving* entails exampling how and why something is wrong. Simply stating that the opposing side is incorrect is not enough. Provide concrete examples and details that *prove* the opposing side is wrong.

CONCLUSION: I'M RIGHT!

Sum up the major points of your argument in the conclusion and end assertively. Remember, you are correct. End strong! Once again, if you began with a personal anecdote, you must revisit, end, and conclude with this anecdote.

> If you begin with a personal anecdote, return to this anecdote in the conclusion.

THE FINAL TOUCHES

Spend the last three minutes proofreading your essay. If you can slip in some vocabulary words (see Chapter 9), it doesn't hurt. Also, make sure to add some *pizzazz*. Include the five elements of style (see Chapter 5) within your essay. This added pizzazz keeps the reader engaged and demonstrates your ability to eloquently express yourself.

Put It All Together: Win the ACT Essay Game

Unlike the SAT, you won't need to do a lot of preparation to memorize topics and choose your examples. Concentrate, instead, on preparing for the test by reviewing the chapters in this book that relate to developing and transitioning your ideas and creating good hooks, rebuttal arguments, and strong closings.

On game day, put all the strategies together and compose a "winning" essay. Each of the following key strategies must be utilized. An organized argument without a conclusion or a stylistic opening without a logical body will not earn you an above-average score!

1. PLAN YOUR ATTACK!

Spend five *full* minutes organizing your argument. Create a small outline in the margin of your paper. Remember, you need to choose a side and prove that your side is correct. Go with the side you can write more points about!

2. BEGIN WITH A BANG! (SEE CHAPTER 5)

Start with an anecdote, a one-word sentence, a thought-provoking question, or a short description to really hook the reader!

3. PRESENT YOUR CASE! (SEE CHAPTER 6)

Make sure to include at least three interesting points in support of your argument.

Start with generalizations and qualify these broad statements with concrete details, examples, and specifics. Keep in mind your audience and avoid juvenile language.

4. BE ASSERTIVE! (SEE CHAPTER 4)

Try to use factual-sounding examples to support your claim. This is a persuasive essay—you want your examples to be *indisputable*. Make sure your language supports your position. Be objective, use a formal tone, and avoid jargon and slang.

5. SHOOT DOWN THE OPPOSITION! (SEE CHAPTER 4)

The winning strategy in any debate, argument, or persuasive essay is to disprove the other side. Choose one or two points from the opposition and shoot these points down.

6. WATCH THE CLOCK

Write for 27-28 minutes and fill two full pages. End your essay. Save a few minutes to review, proofread, and edit your essay and make sure it is legible and neat.

Pump your fists and hum "Eye of the Tiger," champion. You just won over your audience and proved your point.

The following is a sample ACT essay. Try your hand at grading it!

ACT ESSAY PROMPT: *"As the amount of time students spend watching television increases, teachers debate whether television channels should be required to devote at least 20 percent of their programming to educational shows about topics such as science and history. Some teachers support this policy because they think television is an ideal teaching instrument with a very large and very receptive audience. Other teachers do not support this policy because they think what is considered educational by some could be considered merely entertaining by others. In your opinion, should television channels be required to devote at least 20 percent of their programming to educational shows?"*

Very superficial; minimal detail is provided.

I watched as each image flicked across the screen. Ten thousand ants, swarming around a small hill. They were driver ants, and they were hunting—rodents! I couldn't believe my eyes. I've never been a bug person, but these driver ants were so fascinating I simply had to watch. The television show intrigued as well as educated me.

Television too often is seen as a glowing box projecting entertaining sitcoms, dramas and actions. However, this box can also project educational programs as well. Students today spend an increasing amount of time watching television, and some educators are beginning to promote TV watching—so long as channels are devoting 20 percent of their programming to educational shows on service and history. In fact, channels should be required to broadcast educational programs 20 percent of the time.

Clear thesis states the writer's position.

Numerous supporting reasons with clear examples.

If television programming were required to devote at least 20% of their programming to education, then students would be able to choose what to learn about while in the comfort of their own homes. Some people like chemistry, some people like nature, and some people like politics of past presidents. Television is great because it has so many channels to choose from and to learn from.

Good transition.

Another benefit of educational programming is that there would be less stress in learning. For example, there would be no tests or homework, just learning for the sake of learning. Students would be able to focus for thirty minutes or an hour and gain subject-specific information interesting that they find interesting. Also, with television programming

(cont.) Numerous supporting reasons with clear examples.

being more educational, less shows would be about adults partying and being bad influences. Students mimic what they see on the television. When they watch a show like <u>Jersey Shore</u> they might think it's okay to drink and to walk around on the streets ready to punch people. If they watch a history program, on the other hand, it might spark an interest in becoming the president. Finally, educational programming is an ideal way to teach a very large audience without having to dip into school budgets or worry about finding qualified teachers for obscure subjects.

Addresses the opposition.

Some educators believe that television programming is useless because what is considered educational to some may be entertaining to others. This may be true, but isn't it good to be entertained while you learn? If it will keep students from zoning out, then they will be more focused and willing to learn. Education does not equal boredom. In fact, the more engaging and dynamic a lesson, the more effective that lesson can be.

Clearly sets up the rebuttal.

Conclusion restates main arguments and reaffirms position. Ends full circle by connecting to the opening anecdote.

Educational programming is a great way to teach a large audience in an entertaining, stress free way. With the amount of time students spend watching television increasing, television channels should be required to devote at least 20 percent of their programming to education. Although I still don't consider myself a "bug person," without television I would never have realized how interesting insects are. Driver ants have jaws almost as large as their bodies! I never would have been introduced to these ferocious creatures had it not been for television. Hopefully, television is the only place I'll encounter them, though.

COMMENTS: Score 12

This persuasive essay succinctly introduces the issue at hand, takes a clear position, and then logically and coherently defends this position. All supporting reasons are presented upfront, and examples to quantify each reason are also provided. The opposition is addressed and subsequently rebutted, enhancing this essay's persuasiveness. Throughout the essay, readers are reminded of the writer's position, and the conclusion definitively restates this position.

THESIS SENTENCES WORKSHEET

Practice generating thesis sentences to be ready for test day. Below are several SAT essay assignments that relate to the core topics. For each question, respond with a strong thesis statement. Make sure your thesis answers the question and gives specific direction. Obviously, you're not handing this in to be graded, but use the checklist as well as my completed worksheet (see p. 172). Feel free to "borrow" from me and use my examples in your own writing.

- *"Do people learn who they are only when they are forced into action?"*

- *"Should people make more of an effort to keep some things private?"*

- *"Is success in life earned or do people succeed because they are lucky?"*

- *"Would the world be a better place if everyone always told the truth?"*

- *"Should modern society be criticized for being materialistic?"*

- *"Can knowledge be a burden rather than a benefit?"*

- *"Can any obstacle or disadvantage be turned into something good?"*

- *"Do changes that make our lives easier not necessarily make them better?"*

- *"Is it better to change one's attitude than to change one's circumstances?"*

- *"Does outrageous behavior reveal to us the limits of our tolerance?"*

COMPLETED THESIS SENTENCES

"Do people learn who they are only when they are forced into action?"

When disaster strikes and people are faced with obstacles, challenges, and adversity, true character is revealed; both Atticus Finch and Malcolm X exemplify that people learn who they are when forced into action.

"Should people make more of an effort to keep some things private?"

As seen through the actions of Mrs. Dubose in To Kill a Mockingbird and the scandals involving celebrities such as Britney Spears and Tiger Woods, some things are best kept private.

"Is success in life earned or do people succeed because they are lucky?"

The brilliant inventors of the Scientific Revolution and professional athletes such as Michael Jordan show us that success is not serendipitous; rather, it is the result of hard work and dedication.

"Would the world be a better place if everyone always told the truth?"

Although honesty is considered the best policy, sometimes it is best to tell a little white lie in order to benefit others, as seen in Of Mice and Men by John Steinbeck and in my own personal life.

"Should modern society be criticized for being materialistic?"

In the midst of both global and national crises, we can see from the effects of global warming and our economic recession that modern society has become infatuated with luxury and is indeed too materialistic.

"Can knowledge be a burden rather than a benefit?"

Knowledge is a powerful tool that propels mankind toward improvement and acts as a driving force behind creativity, as seen in both the Renaissance and the Scientific Revolution.

"Can any obstacle or disadvantage be turned into something good?"

When things get bad, people tend to focus on what's going wrong at that time. However, as seen during the American Revolution and Mark Twain's The Adventures of Huckleberry Finn, there is always a positive that results from a misfortune.

"Do changes that make our lives easier not necessarily make them better?"

Nuclear power and automobiles are wonderful examples of advancements that make life easier but that are malignant.

"Is it better to change one's attitude than to change one's circumstances?"

The world is a diverse place filled with different people and different ideas. Inevitably, there will be discordance, disagreements, and conflict. Sometimes, though, it is important not to give in and to fight for what you believe in. Both Martin Luther and Atticus Finch from <u>To Kill a Mockingbird</u> show us that it is best to remain true to your beliefs and instead you should try and change your circumstances.

"Does outrageous behavior reveal to us the limits of our tolerance?"

Teachers. Parents. Role models. All of these individuals teach us, guide us and motivate us. However, the greatest lessons we learn, we learn through ourselves and our behavior, as seen through Abigail in <u>The Crucible</u> and King Henry VIII.

TOPIC SENTENCES WORKSHEET

The following worksheet contains weak topic sentences. Re-write each topic sentence to include a main idea and direction. Example answers are on pp. 176-177.

ASSIGNMENT: *"Are people more likely to be productive and successful when they ignore the opinions of others?"*
BAD TOPIC SENTENCE: Martin Luther was a Catholic Monk in the 16th century.
RE-WRITE:

ASSIGNMENT: *"Is it better for people to be realistic or optimistic?"*
BAD TOPIC SENTENCE: The Northerners won the Civil War because they kept fighting.
RE-WRITE:

ASSIGNMENT: *"Is it important to try to understand people's motivations before judging their actions?"*
BAD TOPIC SENTENCE: In <u>To Kill a Mockingbird</u>, Atticus Finch was a lawyer who defended Tom Robinson, a black man.
RE-WRITE:

ASSIGNMENT: *"Is happiness something over which people have no control, or can people choose to be happy?"*
BAD TOPIC SENTENCE: Huck Finn travels every with an escaped slave, Jim.
RE-WRITE:

ASSIGNMENT: *"Do we value only what we struggle for?"*
BAD TOPIC SENTENCE: Women did not get the right to vote until 1920.
RE-WRITE:

ASSIGNMENT: *"Do we learn more from finding out that we have made mistakes or from our successful actions?"*

BAD TOPIC SENTENCE: The bombing of Hiroshima was a huge catastrophe.

RE-WRITE:

ASSIGNMENT: *"Is it true that acting quickly and instinctively is the best response to a crisis?"*

BAD TOPIC SENTENCE: Romeo and Juliet fell in love and ultimately committed suicide.

RE-WRITE:

ASSIGNMENT: *"Do all established traditions deserve to remain in existence?"*

BAD TOPIC SENTENCE: The Catholic Church has been around for centuries.

RE-WRITE:

ASSIGNMENT: *"Is it best not to change our ideas, opinions or behaviors?"*

BAD TOPIC SENTENCE: Galileo invented the telescope during the Scientific Revolution.

RE-WRITE:

ASSIGNMENT: *"Should we admire heroes but not celebrities?"*

BAD TOPIC SENTENCE: Pat Tillman was a professional football star.

RE-WRITE:

COMPLETED TOPIC SENTENCES

The following are weak topic sentences followed by stronger re-writes of the same sentences.

ASSIGNMENT: *"Are people more likely to be productive and successful when they ignore the opinions of others?"*
BAD TOPIC SENTENCE: Martin Luther was a Catholic monk in the 16th century.
RE-WRITE: Martin Luther's blatant opposition to the Catholic Church's selling of indulgences shows us that people should ignore the opinions of others to be most successful.

ASSIGNMENT: *"Is it better for people to be realistic or optimistic?"*
BAD TOPIC SENTENCE: The Northerners won the Civil War because they kept fighting.
RE-WRITE: Although the outlook was grim, the Northerners continued to fight the war against slavery and managed to turn the tides and win the war because of their optimistic determination.

ASSIGNMENT: *"Is it important to try to understand people's motivations before judging their actions?"*
BAD TOPIC SENTENCE: In <u>To Kill a Mockingbird</u>, Atticus Finch was a lawyer who defended Tom Robinson, a black man.
RE-WRITE: Everyone in Maycomb, Alabama, had assumed Tom Robinson guilty of rape because of his skin color—everyone but Atticus Finch, who knew not to prematurely judge another person.

ASSIGNMENT: *"Is happiness something over which people have no control, or can people choose to be happy?"*
BAD TOPIC SENTENCE: Huck Finn travels every with an escaped slave, Jim.
RE-WRITE: Through his relationship with Jim, Huck Finn unintentionally discovered true friendship, the value of trust, and the meaning of happiness.

ASSIGNMENT: *"Do we value only what we struggle for?"*
BAD TOPIC SENTENCE: Women did not get the right to vote until 1920.
RE-WRITE: After almost a century of struggle, women finally received the right to vote—an invaluable liberty—in 1920.

ASSIGNMENT: *"Do we learn more from finding out that we have made mistakes or from our successful actions?"*
BAD TOPIC SENTENCE: After World War I, the entire world was against Germany.
RE-WRITE: As a preventative measure and means of punishment, the world enforced strict

oppressions and heavy taxes on Germany, ultimately leading to the rise of Hitler.

ASSIGNMENT: *"Is it true that acting quickly and instinctively is the best response to a crisis?"*

BAD TOPIC SENTENCE: Romeo and Juliet fell in love and ultimately committed suicide.

RE-WRITE: Romeo and Juliet senselessly committed suicide because they acted too quickly and with too much emotion.

ASSIGNMENT: *"Do all established traditions deserve to remain in existence?"*

BAD TOPIC SENTENCE: The Catholic Church has been around for centuries.

RE-WRITE: The traditions of the Catholic Church, an institute with millennia of history, are sometimes outdated and impractical.

ASSIGNMENT: *"Is it best not to change our ideas, opinions or behaviors?"*

BAD TOPIC SENTENCE: Galileo invented the telescope during the Scientific Revolution.

RE-WRITE: Galileo's invention of the telescope during Europe's Scientific Revolution altered our view of the universe and prompted scientific advancement.

ASSIGNMENT: *"Should we admire heroes but not celebrities?"*

BAD TOPIC SENTENCE: Pat Tillman was a professional football star.

RE-WRITE: Pat Tillman, a professional football player and multi-million dollar athlete, should be admired for his selfless act of patriotism.

BEGIN WITH A BANG WORKSHEET

Engage your reader with style!

Core Topic: Choices

ASSIGNMENT:

"Are we free to make our own decisions or are we limited in the choices we make?"

Template	Your Opening Sentence
Sentence Variety	
Thought-provoking Question	
Repetition	

Core Topic: Competition/Cooperation

ASSIGNMENT:

"Do people have to be highly competitive in order to succeed?"

Template	Your Opening Sentence
Sentence Variety	
Thought-provoking Question	
Repetition	

Core Topic: Conflict	
ASSIGNMENT: *"Does true learning only occur when we experience difficulties?"*	
Template	Your Opening Sentence
Sentence Variety	
Thought-provoking Question	
Repetition	

Core Topic: Conscience/Ethics	
ASSIGNMENT: *"Does being ethical make it hard to be successful?"*	
Template	Your Opening Sentence
Sentence Variety	
Thought-provoking Question	
Repetition	

Core Topic: Creativity	
ASSIGNMENT:	
"Do closed doors make us creative?"	
Template	Your Opening Sentence
Sentence Variety	
Thought-provoking Question	
Repetition	

Core Topic: Group/Individual	
ASSIGNMENT:	
"Is it necessary for people to combine their efforts with those of others in order to be most effective?"	
Template	Your Opening Sentence
Sentence Variety	
Thought-provoking Question	
Repetition	

Core Topic: Happiness	
ASSIGNMENT: *"Is happiness something over which people have no control, or can people choose to be happy?"*	
Template	Your Opening Sentence
Sentence Variety	
Thought-provoking Question	
Repetition	

Core Topic: Heroism	
ASSIGNMENT: *"Should heroes be defined as people who say what they think when we ourselves lack the courage to say it?"*	
Template	Your Opening Sentence
Sentence Variety	
Thought-provoking Question	
Repetition	

Core Topic: Motivation	
ASSIGNMENT: *"Is it better to change one's attitude than to change one's circumstances?"*	
Template	Your Opening Sentence
Sentence Variety	
Thought-provoking Question	
Repetition	

Core Topic: Perfection	
ASSIGNMENT: *"Is perfection something to be admired or sought after?"*	
Template	Your Opening Sentence
Sentence Variety	
Thought-provoking Question	
Repetition	

Core Topic: Perspective/Truth	
ASSIGNMENT: *"Does the truth change depending on perspective?"*	
Template	Your Opening Sentence
Sentence Variety	
Thought-provoking Question	
Repetition	

Core Topic: Sacrifice	
ASSIGNMENT: *"Can what we value be determined only by what we sacrifice?"*	
Template	Your Opening Sentence
Sentence Variety	
Thought-provoking Question	
Repetition	

Core Topic: Success	
ASSIGNMENT: *"Is success in life earned or do people succeed because they are lucky?"*	
Template	Your Opening Sentence
Sentence Variety	
Thought-provoking Question	
Repetition	

Core Topic: Technology	
ASSIGNMENT: *"Do changes that make our lives easier not necessarily make them better?"*	
Template	Your Opening Sentence
Sentence Variety	
Thought-provoking Question	
Repetition	

Core Topic: Wisdom	
ASSIGNMENT: *"What makes a person wise? Are the wisest people merely smart or are they also concerned with the well being of others?"*	
Template	Your Opening Sentence
Sentence Variety	
Thought-provoking Question	
Repetition	

HISTORICAL MOMENTS TEMPLATE CHART

Fill out the chart below, selecting a historical figure, era, and war and include five concrete facts about each so that you'll be prepared for test day. Memorize these facts to OWN your moments!

Figure	Applicable Core Topics
Name:	
Dates:	
Facts	
1.	
2.	
3.	
4.	
5.	

Era	Applicable Core Topics
Name:	
Dates:	
Facts	
1.	
2.	
3.	
4.	
5.	

War	Applicable Core Topics
Name: Dates:	
Facts	
1.	
2.	
3.	
4.	
5.	

LITERATURE TEMPLATE CHART #1

Use these charts to organize your "essay writing facts" for your two literary examples.

Useful Quotes
1.
2.
3.

Core Topic	Relative Details
Choices	1. 2.
Competition/ Cooperation	1. 2.
Conflict	1. 2.
Conscience/ Ethics	1. 2.
Creativity	1. 2.
Group/ Individual	1. 2.
Happiness	1. 2.
Heroism	1. 2.
Motivation	1. 2.

Perfection	1.	
	2.	
Perspective/ Truth	1.	
	2.	
Sacrifice	1.	
	2.	
Success	1.	
	2.	
Wisdom	1.	
	2.	

LITERATURE TEMPLATE CHART #2

Use these charts to organize your "essay writing facts" for your two literary examples.

Useful Quotes
1.
2.
3.

Core Topic	Relative Details
Choices	1. 2.
Competition/ Cooperation	1. 2.
Conflict	1. 2.
Conscience/ Ethics	1. 2.
Creativity	1. 2.
Group/ Individual	1. 2.
Happiness	1. 2.
Heroism	1. 2.
Motivation	1. 2.

Perfection	1.	
	2.	
Perspective/ Truth	1.	
	2.	
Sacrifice	1.	
	2.	
Success	1.	
	2.	
Wisdom	1.	
	2.	

CURRENT EVENTS TEMPLATE CHART

Use the chart below to organize your current event details for test day.

Event	Applicable Core Topics
Details	
1.	
2.	
3.	
4.	
5.	

Event	Applicable Core Topics
Details	
1.	
2.	
3.	
4.	
5.	

Event	Applicable Core Topics
Details	
1.	
2.	
3.	
4.	
5.	

SPORTS TEMPLATE CHART

Use the chart below to organize your sports moment/athlete details for test day.

Sports Moment/Athlete	Applicable Core Topics
Details	
1.	
2.	
3.	
4.	
5.	

Sports Moment/Athlete	Applicable Core Topics
Details	
1.	
2.	
3.	
4.	
5.	

Sports Moment/Athlete	Applicable Core Topics
Details	
1.	
2.	
3.	
4.	
5.	

PERSONAL EXPERIENCE TEMPLATE CHART

Use the chart below to organize your personal experience details for test day.

Pivotal Moment	Applicable Core Topics
Details	
1.	
2.	
3.	
4.	
5.	

Pivotal Moment	Applicable Core Topics
Pivotal Moment	
1.	
2.	
3.	
4.	
5.	

Pivotal Moment	Applicable Core Topics
Details	
1.	
2.	
3.	
4.	
5.	

Laura Wilson, M.A., is the founder and CEO of the nationally recognized online test-preparation company, WilsonDailyPrep, and of WilsonPrep, a premier tutoring agency in Chappaqua, New York. In addition to more than twenty years of teaching English and tutoring high-school students for the SAT and ACT, she regularly consults closely with other English teachers, supervising and mentoring them in the classroom. She often consults with school districts, using her original curriculum guides to infuse grammar, reading, and writing skills into the study of high-school literary classics. In 2010, she founded Graph It Forward Today, an organization that donates graphing calculators to students and schools in need. In addition to *Write the SAT Essay Right*, her first Maupin House book, she is the author of *The WilsonDailyPrep Verbal Workbook*, *The WilsonDailyPrep Math Workbook*, and *English in English*. She lives in Chappaqua, New York, with her husband, Mike, and her sons, Mitchell and Max.

The author would like to acknowledge the contributions and support of Amie Whigham.

Amie Whigham has a background in science and education. She has been a teacher and tutor at both the high school and college levels, and recognizes the need for engaging, dynamic instruction at even the most advanced level of learning. Finding a voice as a writer and strengthening composite writing skills can be a laborious process. Collaborating with Laura Wilson in writing *Write the SAT Essay Right*, Amie hoped to animate this process and make eloquent writing an accessible skill to students of all abilities.